D0059771

THE NAMES OF
GOD

KEN HEMPHILL

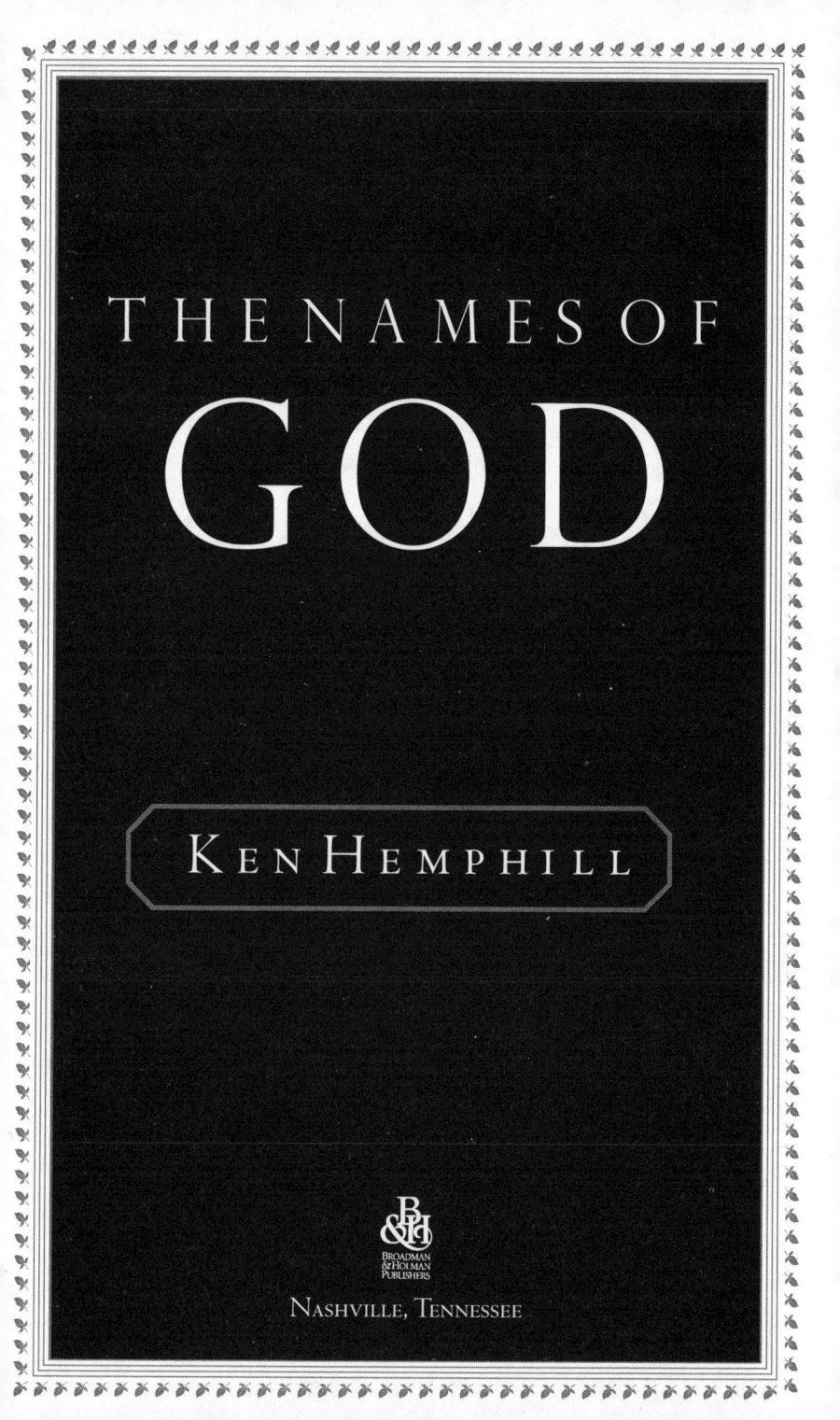

BROADMAN
&HOLMAN
PUBLISHERS

NASHVILLE, TENNESSEE

© 2001 by Kenneth S. Hemphill
All rights reserved
Printed in the United States of America

0-8054-2436-9

Published by Broadman & Holman Publishers,
Nashville, Tennessee

Dewey Decimal Classification: 231
Subject Heading: CHRISTIAN LIVING/BIBLE STUDY
Library of Congress Card Catalog Number: 00-068090

Unless otherwise stated, all Scripture used is from the NASB, the New
American Standard Bible, © the Lockman Foundation, 1960, 1962,
1963, 1968, 1971, 1972, 1973, 1975, 1977, 1995; used by permission.
Other versions used include the NKJV, New King James Version, copy-
right © 1979, 1980, 1982, Thomas Nelson, Inc., Publishers.

Library of Congress Cataloging-in-Publication Data

Hemphill, Kenneth S., 1948-
    The names of God / Kenneth S. Hemphill
        p. cm.
    ISBN 0-8054-2436-9
    1. God—Name. 2. God—Name—Biblical teaching. I. Title.

BT180.N2 H46 2001
213—dc21

                                                    00-068090

            6 7 8 9 10   03 04 05 06

To my daughter Katherine,
A joyous and energetic follower of Christ,
On the celebration of your graduation
And journey to university.
My prayer is that your
Pilgrimage of faith will always
Be a serendipitous discovery of
The sufficiency of our God.

CONTENTS

Foreword   ix

Acknowledgments   xi

Introduction   1

Chapter 1: Elohim   9

Chapter 2: Adonai   21

Chapter 3: El Elyon   35

Chapter 4: El Shaddai   49

Chapter 5: Yahweh   63

Chapter 6: Jehovah Jireh   79

Chapter 7: Jehovah Rophe   91

Chapter 8: Jehovah Nissi   105

Chapter 9: Jehovah Mekadesh   119

Chapter 10: Jehovah Shalom   133

Chapter 11: Jehovah Tsidkenu   147

Chapter 12: Jehovah Rohi   161

Chapter 13: Jehovah Shammah   177

Chapter 14: The Growing Relationship   193

FOREWORD

The Scriptures reveal not one, but many names for God the Father, God the Son, and God the Holy Spirit. Though One is essence, God's characteristics are revealed throughout the Bible by the descriptive names He chose to use in intimate relationship with His people.

This priceless treasure of His character, as revealed in His names, shows us how wonderful, powerful, and loving He really is. But, as you will see in these pages, God has not only given us His name; He has also instructed us how to draw upon its teachings in our daily walk with our Lord and Savior, Jesus Christ.

Dr. Ken Hemphill has used his unique ability to weave God's names and characteristics to challenge and inspire the reader to deeper faith and commitment. Every inspiring chapter focuses on the hope of God's Word and how we can use it when we need it most.

Dr. Robert C. Hill, President
Hillwood Ministries

I am indebted to Dr. Robert C. Hill for his masterful work on this book with me. Dr. Hill died on December 5, 2000. He was an active member of the Southwestern Advisory Council at Southwestern Baptist Theological Seminary. Bob dedicated his life to ministry. One of the last acts of his ministry here with us was shepherding this book to publication. We will miss him very much.

Dr. Kenneth Hemphill
President, Southwestern Baptist Theological Seminary

ACKNOWLEDGMENTS

This book has been a joy and a pilgrimage. I first preached a series on the names of God in 1990, while I was pastor at the First Baptist Church of Norfolk, Virginia. The study and the messages had a profound and lasting impact on me. The response of the congregation greatly encouraged me as they testified to a new awareness of God's sufficiency for daily living. Soon after I preached the series, I left First Norfolk to become the founding director of the Center for Church Growth under the auspices of the Home Mission and Sunday School Boards of the Southern Baptist Convention. (Now the North American Mission Board and LifeWay Christian Resources, respectively.) After two years' service in that capacity, the Lord led me to Fort Worth, Texas, to assume the presidency of Southwestern Baptist Theological Seminary. The understanding I have gained of the character and nature of God has daily sustained me through this transitional period in my life. I have frequently been reminded of God's sufficiency as I have called to remembrance the various names of God. While serving as interim pastor at First Baptist Church of Dallas, Texas, I had the occasion to preach the sermon series that is the foundational study for the content of this book. The good folks at First Dallas encouraged me to put this material into print for a broader audience. This book is a labor of love and a gift of love to two wonderful church families.

I could say thanks to a countless number of folks who have helped with this process. Of course I am grateful to the two congregations that provided personal feedback concerning the messages as they were delivered. For my original sermon series, I was greatly inspired by the book *Names of God,* by Nathan Stone.

Anyone familiar with Stone's book will recognize the tremendous debt I owe to this great scholar. While the manuscript was in process, several Old Testament specialists gave their time to look at various parts. Gene Merrill of Dallas Theological Seminary and Boo Heflin and George Klein of Southwestern Seminary have been gracious to offer advice when solicited. Let me be quick to add that any flaws of exegesis that remain are solely the fault of the author, who remains somewhat of a novice in Old Testament exegesis. Barbara Walker, my administrative assistant, has rendered invaluable aid in formatting my rough drafts of each chapter.

I would like to thank the Southwestern Advisory Council, who encouraged the seminary to pursue this project and who assist Southwestern Seminary in countless ways to fulfill its God-given task.

As always, my most profound thanks go to my wife, Paula, who is my helpmate, fellow laborer, and sounding board. She has listened to the messages behind this book on more than one occasion and given valuable input.

I pray that the Lord will receive glory through this book and that you will grow in His likeness as your understanding of His character is deepened and broadened.

INTRODUCTION

Can you remember the agonizing struggle to name your first child? You wanted to choose a name that wouldn't cause your grown child to question your early sanity. You also had to think about the feelings of all the relatives who were hoping that someone in the family would name a child after them. Paula and I were living in Cambridge, England, when Kristina, our eldest, was born. I was a graduate student at the University, and we were facing the impending birth without the advantage of wise counsel from parents living nearby. We had selected two different girl's names. My wife was partial to one and I, of course, wanted the other. Curiously, we didn't even select a name for a boy, but that has proved never to be a problem, since we are the proud parents of three girls. Truthfully, with Kristina, we didn't decide until the morning of her birth as we held her in our arms and looked into her face. In that moment, we knew that her name would be Kristina.

Why all the hassle? Why do we struggle so intensely in the naming of a child? What's in a name anyway? Johnny Cash surely "cashed" in on that question with his song, "A Boy Named Sue." In that song, an absentee father named his son "Sue" so that he would have to learn to defend himself.

Names are important because they are a method of self-revelation. When we meet people, our first question usually is, "What's your name?" Most of us have several names to which we will respond. In some contexts, I'm called Dr. Hemphill. In most instances, I am simply called Ken. My favorite, of course, is Daddy. My girls have a way of saying that name that melts my resolve and opens the floodgates of my wallet. Occasionally,

I am called Honey. Once, while in England, I received a letter from a man in Germany who spelled out my name with all its corresponding titles. The envelope was addressed to "The Right Reverend Herr Professor Doctor Doctor Ken Hemphill." I was so amazed with my high-sounding label that I saved the letter for a long while. It served as somewhat of a counterbalance for some of the other names I've been called.

MEANING OF NAMES

The way various names and titles are used speaks of relationships. Those who know me only in a work relationship might refer to me as Dr. Hemphill. People who know me more personally usually call me Ken. Only my children call me Daddy. Even though we assign great significance to names and titles today, they were far more important to the men and women of the ancient Near East during biblical times. For them, the very existence of a thing was tied up with the revelation of its name. For example, think of the creation narrative. Adam's stewardship came first of all in naming the animals. This duty was intricately related to the truth that the animals had been created for his provision. He was steward over them, so he had the authority to give them their names.

The name *Jacob,* "the deceiver," was changed to *Israel* as he wrestled with the angel. The prophetic pathos in the naming of the children of Hosea cannot be overlooked. The first child was named *Jezreel,* which meant "God sows." The second child was *Lo-Ruhamah,* which meant "no more compassion." Finally, the third child was named *Lo-Ammi,* which meant "not my people." When you read the prophetic Book of Hosea, you will see that the names of the children were pregnant with meaning concerning God's judgment upon His people.

The divine name was critically important in the ancient Near East. The one who knew the divine name was able to invoke the presence and obtain the help of deity. Jacob understood the significance of the divine name, and therefore as he wrestled with the angel, he pleaded with his nighttime attacker to tell him his name (Gen. 32:24–32). Moses, when he was confronted by God at the burning bush, was given a commission to deliver Israel from bondage. Moses argued with God, saying that no one would believe him. Listen to the text: "Then Moses said to God, 'Behold, I am going to the sons of Israel, and I shall say to them, "The God of your fathers has sent me to you," Now they may say to me, "What is His name?" What shall I say to them?'" (Exod. 3:13).

THREE REASONS TO STUDY THE NAMES

As we begin this study on the names of God, I want to do a little background research with you first. We must ask the question, "Why do we need to study the names of God? What difference will it make in our personal walk with Him?"

The Commandment to Honor the Name

The first thing to remember is that God has commanded us to honor His name. Exodus 20:7 simply states: "You shall not take the name of the LORD your God in vain." Isn't it interesting that God gave us only ten commandments and one of them focused on His name? The commandment means more than avoiding using God's name in a slang or profane way. It means that those who are in relationship with Him must honor His name in their lives. The name of God has to do with His character, and when we live in covenant relationship with Him, we become accountable for reflecting His character.

I vividly remember the last few moments before I left for Wake Forest University to report for freshman football practice. Our family was very close and I realized that it would be an emotional departure. Mom didn't want to come outside to tell me good-bye, so we said our farewells in the kitchen and Dad walked me down to the car. I was mentally prepared for him to recite a list of rules and regulations to govern my life in college. But my Dad outsmarted me. As we walked to the car, he put his hand on my shoulder and said, "Son, I've only got one piece of advice."

I thought, "Amen, I'm gonna make it out of here today."

"Son, I've only got one thing of value to give you and that's my name." He paused for a moment to let that sink in, then added, "Don't take my name anywhere I wouldn't take it, and don't do anything with my name that I wouldn't do with it. That's my only request as you go off to college."

Need I tell you the consequences of that request? I had friends whose parents had laid down all the rules in a long list before they left for college. The only problem was that the rules couldn't cover all the potential sin that was available to a young person in college. Many of these individuals participated in behavior they knew wouldn't be approved of by their parents, but they did so with abandon because they had no specific rule to prohibit it. I, on the other hand, was able to stand against sin in that place of temptation because of my dad's simple admonition.

When my friends would say, "Let's go here," or "Let's do this," I would then ask myself, "Would my dad do that or would he go to that place?" I knew that I couldn't participate in many activities because Dad had entrusted me with his name.

Do you realize that when you are in Christ, you bear His name? Your behavior reflects upon Him. When we take the name *Christian,* we must remember the commandment that says, "You shall not take the name of the LORD your God in vain" (Exod. 20:7a).

The Praise Factor

Another reason to study the names of God is simply because of the inherent greatness of His name. Psalm 8:1 says:

> O LORD, our Lord,
> How majestic is Thy name in all the earth . . .

In Psalm 48:10, the psalmist states:

> As is Thy name O God,
> So is Thy praise to the ends of the earth; . . .

The psalmist Asaph frequently begins his praise of God with a reference to His name. Look, for example, at the first verse of Psalm 75:

> We give thanks to Thee, O God, we give thanks,
> For Thy name is near;
> Men declare Thy wondrous works.

He begins Psalm 76 by saying:

> God is known in Judah;
> His name is great in Israel.

Understanding the names of God will help us to understand how to praise and worship Him more effectively. For this reason alone, as believers we should hunger to understand the significance of the names of God. His name is great and He is worthy of our praise. Like an earthly father, He must rejoice when He hears his children praise Him with the use of His name.

The Protection of the Name

A third important reason for us to know the names of God is found in Proverbs 18:10, which says, "The name of the LORD is a strong tower; / The righteous runs into it and is safe." In other words, God's name is like a fort that provides protection for the believer. Through this study, we will come to understand the significance of names like *Jehovah Rophe* or *Jehovah Nissi*. In each case, we will learn how understanding that name becomes a spiritual fortress. For example, we will discover that *Jehovah Rophe* can bring healing, thus turning bitter experiences into sweet. We will find that *Jehovah Nissi* is a banner of protection that can give us spiritual victory. We will discover that *Jehovah Jireh* is a God of infinite provision who can meet every need of our lives.

As we grow to understand the very nature and character of God, we will find ourselves running to His name to find safety and strength. His name is like a strong tower! God's name stands for the manifestation of His presence in His revelation and His relation to His people. This can be one of the most exciting and encouraging studies that you have ever undertaken.

It is essential to know God's name because we bear that name and we are commanded to live in such a way that will bring it honor. As we come to know the significance of each name, we will enhance the breadth of our ability to praise God and to live in His protection.

THREE FOUNDATIONAL PRINCIPLES

Before we study the first name given in Genesis 1:1 we also need to cover three important foundational principles. These principles will help us to keep the overall significance of the revelation of the names of God in view as we study the individual names.

A Gift from a Loving Father

The names for God that we will study are names that God revealed to us. That's a rather critical issue to aid our understanding of the Old Testament. They are not the creation of men who were trying to define and describe God. Indeed, we will discover that they are sometimes given in response to a direct question. For example, the name *Yahweh* (Jehovah) was revealed to Moses when he asked God in Exodus 3 whom he should say had sent him. In other instances, God simply declared His name. When Abraham was prepared to sacrifice Isaac, God revealed Himself to be *Jehovah Jireh,* the God who provides.

God in His infinite mercy has revealed Himself on the stage of human history that we might come to know Him in a personal relationship. As God reveals Himself, He discloses His character and nature through the expression of His names.

The Key to a Growing Relationship

By giving His name, God demonstrates His desire to know and to be known by us. He is a God who reveals Himself so that we can know Him personally. As we look at these names, take note of the opportunity they reveal to have an intimate and growing relationship with God. As we study each name, ask yourself, "Do I know God in my own life to be the manifestation of this truth?" For example, do you know Him as *Jehovah Nissi,* the banner of victory in your life? If you can say that you *understand* this promise of victory, then ask yourself whether you have *appropriated* that victory.

In another section, we will discover that He is *Adonai,* which means Lord. We easily and frequently call Him Lord, but does our life reveal that we have relinquished all issues of ownership? To a people in captivity, God reveals Himself as *Jehovah Shammah,* the Lord is there (Ezek. 48:35b). The prophet Ezekiel looks forward to the day when God's temple will be rebuilt. His is a message of hope and restoration—Israel will once again know His presence. The progressive revelation of God's names will lead us on a spiritual pilgrimage to discover a growing relationship with the sovereign God of the universe. The order in which the Bible reveals the names is not as important as what each name tells us about God's character. *God reveals Himself fully so that we might experience His fullness.*

The Character of God Displayed

Each one of God's names reveals another aspect of His multi-faceted character. In Psalm 23, David says: "He guides me in the paths of righteousness / For His name's sake" (v. 3). That phrase does not mean that God is acting to save His reputation. What it means is that God is acting in conformity with His own nature. That is, God leads in paths of righteousness because He is by nature a righteous God. This glorious truth means that we can joyfully and confidently follow Him, because we know that He is righteous and thus could not lead us in paths that would be injurious to us. What a contrast between the God of truth and revelation and the gods of mythology, who were often depicted as being deceptive.

As we study each name, you will learn something more about the lovely character of our God. You will discover that He is our Provider, Sustainer, Healer, Shepherd, and more. You will find yourself intimately drawn to Him and passionately committed to Him. You will find that surrender to His Lordship is sheer joy, for you will know His character and trust Him to act in your life according to His character.

I

ELOHIM

POWERFUL GOD

In the beginning God created the heavens
and the earth.

GENESIS 1:1

The Bible begins with a simple but profound declaration of faith—in the beginning there was only God, nothing else. Everything else that comes to be comes as the result of the activity of God.

GOD ALONE IS ETERNAL

The name used in Genesis 1:1 is *Elohim*. In its context, it is a declaration that God alone is eternal. We can thus declare that nature is not eternal. It did not exist until God declared that it would exist. The evangelical church has long proclaimed its conviction that God created out of nothing ("ex nihilo") everything that is. This critical and fundamental premise of Scripture stands in sharp contrast to a humanistic evolutionary model, which ultimately ends up claiming that matter or the universe is infinitely old. In a humanistic system, the universe becomes godlike, creating life out of lifeless matter through some mindless, random system. In affirming that God alone is eternal and is the creator of all that exists, we find that Scripture gives ultimate dignity and meaning to human life and existence. We can know that life has meaning and purpose. If we are to discover that purpose, we must know the one who alone is eternal, our Creator. Further, it lays open the possibility that we can have eternal life. Mankind has always sought to find the secret to life after death, to eternal life. But it's no secret! Eternal life can only be found in relationship to God, who is eternal.

THE SIGNIFICANCE OF THE PLURAL

The name used for God in Genesis 1:1 is from the Hebrew *Elohim*. Elohim is the plural form of the simpler name *El* or

Eloah (the root is debated by scholars). It is the name most frequently used for God in the Old Testament. The name El, probably means "first" as in "Lord," and indicates that God is the strong and mighty one. The singular name El is not often used alone in the Old Testament. El is most frequently found in compound names such as *El Shaddai,* or *El Elyon.*

There is some debate among scholars as to the significance in the use of the plural Elohim. Look, for example, at Genesis 1:26, where Elohim is used with the plural pronouns *us* and *our:* "Then God said, 'Let Us make man in Our image, according to Our likeness . . . ' "

Some Bible teachers argue that the use of the plural Elohim points to the triune nature of God. From the very beginning, God, who is eternal in His nature, has always been three in one. There's only one true God, but He manifests Himself in His plurality as God the Father, God the Son, and God the Holy Spirit.

We refer to this as the doctrine of the Trinity. The concept is found throughout Scripture. For example, we find Paul ending the second Corinthian letter with this benediction: "The grace of the Lord Jesus Christ, and the love of God, and the fellowship of the Holy Spirit, be with you all." In the glorious prayer that begins the Letter to the Ephesians (1:3–14) we find all three persons of the Godhead as they are related to our experience of salvation.

Although the concept of the triune nature of God is clearly taught throughout the Scriptures, the plural use of Elohim does not in and of itself confirm the existence of the Trinity. We can assert, however, that the plural Elohim allows for subsequent trinitarian revelation.

Other Bible teachers argue that the plural Elohim may have simply had an intensifying sense, indicating God's majesty in the fullness of His power. Thus, when Israel confessed the name

Elohim, they were acknowledging that God contained within Himself all the divine attributes. It was a solemn confession that He alone is the one supreme and true God and that He is personally knowable. While it may be difficult to assert with full confidence that the plural was intended to point to the triune nature of God, we can be assured that both of these truths are taught within Scripture. Our God, the God of creation, is the one true God who contains within Himself all of divinity. To provide for our salvation, He has revealed Himself as God the Father, God the Son, and God the Holy Spirit.

THE CREATOR

Genesis 1:1 clearly affirms that Elohim was the maker of the heavens and the earth. As we look at the names of God, in each case it will be in the context in which they were first revealed. Therefore, we will do a brief survey of the Old Testament.

It is interesting, and important, to note that the first thing God wanted us to know about Himself is that He is the Creator of the heavens and the earth. The early church saw the doctrine of creation as central to faith. The church faced a pagan world that believed the universe was eternal, and that whatever gods existed, they were finite parts of this universe. As you study church history, you will find that many of the hymns and creeds of the church expressed the bedrock certainty that God was the Creator of all that exists. The doctrine of creation was viewed as the beginning point of theology. If you know the Apostles' Creed, you realize that belief in the Creator is a basic tenet of that confession.

Some years ago, I was teaching as a guest professor on one of our seminary campuses. Carl F. H. Henry, one of the great evangelical thinkers of our generation, was also teaching there at the same time. One evening, several of the guest professors were invited to the president's home along with several resident faculty members. During a casual dinner conversation, the president of the school inquired, "Dr. Henry, are you writing anything special at the moment?"

If you know anything of the prolific nature of Dr. Henry's writing, you would understand the significance of the question and of his response. He responded that he was writing a small book that might well be the most important contribution he had made to evangelical scholarship. You can imagine how that response focused our attention on what had begun as casual conversation.

The president continued by asking about the book's thesis.

I will never forget Dr. Henry's response, because it challenged me to reexamine my own thinking. He stated that it was his conviction that evangelical scholarship had veered off track when they quit believing and defending the historical truth of the doctrine of creation. He stated that once the evangelical community jettisoned the historical reliability of the creation narratives, they began to lose confidence in other great doctrinal truths. He then challenged us to teach this truth as a bedrock reality of our faith.

The truth of God's creative acts in Genesis was foundational to the early church's belief and witness. It is still the core essential for our belief today. In contrast to the evolutionary model which is foundational to pagan, humanistic, and New Age philosophies, we can declare that everything that exists was the act of a sovereign, loving, and knowable God. He made everything that is, including us. That means we have unique purpose. We are here by design and by divine providence.

I love to talk with teenagers about the beautiful truth that God created. So many of our youth believe that their lives are nothing more than the result of a chance evolutionary process. Some feel that they were unwanted by their parents. I can say to them without any equivocation, "Listen, I want you to know that no matter what you have heard, God formed you in your mother's womb. He uniquely knit you together from the very beginning, and He knows your name."

He is the sovereign God of the universe. All the other attributes of God are based on this affirmation that He existed prior to, is independent of, and sovereign over His creation—that the world itself reflects His glory. Historically, the church based its theology on that doctrine, for it is the most mysterious, most incomprehensible doctrine in the Bible. What human mind can fathom the act of creation? How could God bring everything from out of nothing? How do you make life from nonlife? The inspired writers of Scripture stood in awe of the Creator God, as we should today.

Do you remember the story of Job? Job finds himself in a predicament that he could not understand. From all the outward circumstances, it appears that life has dealt him a cruel blow. All of his wealth and family has been taken from him. His friends advise him to curse God and die. Toward the end of the book, we have the account of Job calling into question the nature and actions of God. God patiently and lovingly responds to him with a litany of questions:

> "Where were you when I laid the foundation of
> the earth!
> Tell Me, if you have understanding,
> Who set its measurements, since you know?
> Or who stretched the line on it?" (Job 38:4–5)

The questions about the creation and preservation continue from chapter 38 to chapter 41. God graciously reminds Job that he is the created and that God is the Creator. The created cannot fully fathom the work of the Creator, yet he can trust Him. If God has faithfully provided for the beasts of the field, He can and will provide for man, who was created in His image. God declares to Job, I know you, I can sustain you, and I can care for you. You can trust me.

Job's confession in chapter 42 is the beginning of the transformation in his attitude about life;

> "I know that Thou canst do all things,
> And that no purpose of Thine can be thwarted. . . .
> 'Hear, now, and I will speak;
> I will ask Thee, and do Thou instruct me.'
> I have heard of Thee by the hearing of the ear;
> But now my eye sees Thee;
> Therefore I retract,
> And I repent in dust and ashes." (42:2, 4–6)

Job's personal understanding of God as creator of all that is restores his confidence that He can provide for his everyday needs. This leads Job to a repentant and humble position before the loving, sovereign Creator of the earth.

The understanding that God is Elohim, the Creator and Sustainer of all that exists, gives us confidence to face life's difficulties. As we place our trust in Him through His Son, Jesus Christ, we know that He who created us can sustain us. This wonderful truth when fully comprehended helps you overcome fear and anxiety in everyday living.

THE BEAUTIFUL ASSURANCES

I've heard some people say, "I wouldn't have such trouble believing the Bible if I could just cut out the first couple of chapters. I find them very difficult to believe." What a tragic misunderstanding. First, even if they could remove the first couple of chapters, they would still have difficulty with the Bible, because references to the creative activity of God are found throughout the Word of God. But, even more, they would miss the beautiful assurances found in the truth that God is our Creator.

Let's look at just a small sampling of the wonderful assurances that God is our Creator. Look first at Isaiah 40:26:

> Lift up your eyes on high
> And see who has created these stars,
> The One who leads forth their host by number,
> He calls them all by name;
> Because of the greatness of His might and the
>   strength of His power
> Not one of them is missing.

What Isaiah is saying is that God both created and sustains the universe. On the basis of this great truth, God asks why Israel would think that God doesn't know about their needs and doesn't give them justice (v. 27). God responds:

> Do you not know? Have you not heard?
> The Everlasting God, the LORD, the Creator of
>   the ends of the earth
> Does not become weary or tired.
> His understanding is inscrutable.
> He gives strength to the weary.
> And to him who lacks might He increases power.

This section ends with a verse you may have committed to memory:

> Yet those who wait for the LORD
> Will gain new strength;
> They will mount up with wings like eagles,
> They will run and not get tired,
> They will walk and not become weary. (40:31)

The Creator does not become weary and He gives strength to us for the living of everyday life.

Another assuring passage is Isaiah 42:5:

> Thus says God the LORD,
> Who created the heavens and stretched them out,
> Who spread out the earth and its offspring,
> Who gives breath to the people on it,
> And spirit to those who walk in it.

Isaiah tells us that God is the source of all life, and therefore we can know that life is sacred. We can know that we are special to God. Isaiah 43:1 echoes this same great assurance with reference to the creative activity of God.

In Isaiah 45:11–13, the prophet Isaiah points to the creative activity of God to confirm that God is indeed in control of history:

> Thus says the LORD, the Holy One of Israel, and his Maker:
> "Ask Me about the things to come concerning My sons,
> And you shall commit to Me the work of My hands.

It is I who made the earth, and created man upon
   it." (vv. 11–12a)

Based on this essential truth, God promises the release of the
exiles and the building of the city (v. 13). Isaiah affirms that the
God of creation is also in control of history and therefore Israel
need not fret. Only God has the power to tell them the things
that are to come.

I attended college during the turbulent years of the Vietnam
War. Some on campus believed that we were experiencing the
beginning of the end. Others were simply frustrated by current
events and believed that all of history was spinning madly out of
control. Remember how so many people feared that the Y2K
disaster would send the world into economic chaos? Millions of
dollars are being spent on psychic hotlines by those who desire
to know the future. I cannot predict what will happen with
whatever today's world crisis is, nor do I have any secret insight
into the stock market. I can, however, assure you that none of
these events will take the creator unaware. Only He knows and
controls the universe.

People today are concerned about the fragmenting of our
society. People are looking for a way to heal broken relationships. Look at Malachi 2:10: "'Do we not all have one father?
Has not one God created us? Why do we deal treacherously each
against his brother so as to profane the covenant of our
fathers?'" Since God created us, He is Father of all of us.
Therefore He provides the common ground for building and
healing relationships. Relationships between men and women,
the nations of the world, the rich and the poor would be radically altered by the understanding that we all have one Father.
We know that the sinful condition of man's heart has radically

altered God's created purpose for mankind. The sin problem can only be resolved through Christ, who provides access to the Father. Thus Paul could declare that for the Christian, "There is neither Jew nor Greek, there is neither slave nor free man, there is neither male nor female; for you are all one in Christ Jesus" (Gal. 3:28). The relational unity established by the Creator has been restored in Christ.

As in Genesis, so in the Book of Revelation, the last book of the Bible, you will find a focus on the doctrine of creation. The Book of Revelation is a wonderful book of praise. Look at 10:5–6 where one of the angelic host is preparing to praise the Lord. "And the angel whom I saw standing on the sea and on the land lifted up his right hand to heaven, and swore by Him who lives forever and ever, WHO CREATED HEAVEN AND THE THINGS IN IT, AND THE EARTH AND THE THINGS IN IT, AND THE SEA AND THE THINGS IN IT . . ." From Genesis to Revelation, God is presented to us as Elohim, the God of creation.

WHAT THIS MEANS

What does God being the God of creation mean? First of all, it means that you have been created in the image of a personal God. Among other things, this means that you are relational, rational, and responsible. You have been created to enjoy a personal relationship with your Creator and your fellow man. Yet we realize that all of these relationships have been radically altered by our sin. The Bible tells us that all have sinned and have fallen short of the glory of God. Further we are told that the wages of this sin is death (Rom. 3:23 and 6:23). Death refers not only to our ultimate physical death, but also to immediate spiritual death. This spiritual death separates all of mankind from their holy Creator.

But the Bible contains incredible good news. The Creator is also the Redeemer. In a radical act of compassion and grace, the Creator entered into His creation to redeem fallen man. This is the only way redemption could have occurred. Your Creator took upon Himself human flesh and gave Himself to pay the penalty for your sin so that you could be restored to an intimate relationship with Him (2 Cor. 5:21). You are a rational being. You can fully understand these wonderful truths. Further, you are responsible; you must make a decision to commit your life to Christ. Listen to Romans 10:9–10: "That if you confess with your mouth Jesus *as* Lord, and believe in your heart that God raised Him from the dead, you shall be saved; for with the heart man believes, resulting in righteousness, and with the mouth he confesses, resulting in salvation."

Where do you stand in your relationship with your Creator? Perhaps you only know Him as Creator. You can know Him personally as your Redeemer. If you have never made this wonderful discovery, you can do so right now. Why not simply but honestly invite Him to forgive your sin and come into your life. You can pray such a prayer in your own words.

Second, you can be assured that your life itself has purpose and design. News sources reveal that teen suicide is on the increase—it is the second leading killer of teenagers today. According to the suicide notes they leave, many teens tell us they have chosen to end their lives because they have come to the conclusion that life has no purpose. Nothing could be further from the truth. Whether you are a teenager, senior adult, or young adult, *you have purpose.* Every person is created by design and has purpose in life.

2

ADONAI

LORD

But Abram said, "Lord GOD, what will
You give me, seeing I go childless, and the
heir of my house is Eliezer of Damascus?"

GENESIS 15:2, NKJV

Have you ever heard someone say, or have you ever been tempted yourself to say, "I am the master of my own fate, the author of my destiny!" This is a common misconception that goes back to the Garden of Eden and is one of the greatest lies promoted by our adversary, the devil. We were all created by a loving God who has a purpose for our lives.

Adonai, usually translated as "Lord" in the English text, generally has a capital *L* followed by *ord* in small letters. The name *Yahweh,* which we will study later, is translated with the word "LORD" in all upper case letters.

Adonai occurs nearly 300 times in the Old Testament. It is used some 215 times in reference to men. When it is used in reference to man, it may mean "sir," as a title of respect, or it can mean "master," or "lord." When it is used in reference to people, it is always in the singular, *Adon.*

When Adonai is used for God, it is used in the plural. Some commentators argue that the plural used for the name of God is another implicit suggestion in the Old Testament of the triune nature of God, who reveals Himself as God the Father, God the Son, and God the Holy Spirit. However, it is possible that the plural Adonai is used to enhance, or underline and exalt, the awesome majesty of God. In either case, we will find that this name Adonai offers a challenge to His followers to recognize His Lordship in our lives.

GOD IS OWNER OF ALL THAT EXISTS

The primary significance of the name Adonai is that of ownership. The truth is that God is the rightful owner of every member of the human family and thus can rightly require our worship and obedience.

We have a powerful illustration of the emphasis on owner-ship in the Old Testament Book of Malachi, which was written to call Israel to repentance for their brazen and callous behavior. They had divorced their wives, they had polluted their worship, they had robbed God of the tithe, which was consecrated unto God. Israel had trampled God's Word under their feet in blatant disobedience.

The questions posed by God, as recorded in Malachi 1:6, are designed to call Israel to repentance. """A son honors his father, and a servant his master. Then if I am a father, where is My honor? And if I am a master, where is My respect?" says the LORD of hosts to you, O priests who despise My name. But you say, "How have we despised Thy name?"'" Two forms of the root from which we get Adonai appear in this text with different suf-fixes. God tells the nation of Israel that it is to be expected that a son honors his father and a servant his master. Then He inquires concerning the lack of honor shown to Him as both Father and Master. The priests, who were to be serving Him, had actually dishonored His name by offering defiled food on His altar (1:7).

Instead of bringing a pure and acceptable sacrifice, they would search among their herd and bring animals that were lame and sick. Their callous offering of the useless animals of their flock was a reproach to God, who was the Lord of all and whose name should be revered among the nations. If you read the first chapter of Malachi you will find six explicit references to His name. His name is holy and deserves highest honor, but the priests have brought reproach upon His name by failing to acknowledge His ownership of all that exists. Their willingness to offer less than the best in sacrifice to God demonstrates their failure to honor His name and recognize His authority as Master and owner of all. The first chapter ends with a great declaration:

"... I am a great King," says the Lord of hosts, "and My name is feared among the nations."

Adonai Declares God's Ownership

The first usage of Adonai is found in Genesis 15:2. We begin the story of the life of Abram with God's call and promise of a blessing in chapter 12. God calls Abram to leave his country and settle a land that He will show him. The promised blessing is recorded in Genesis 12:2:

> "And I will make you a great nation,
> And I will bless you,
> And make your name great;
> And so you shall be a blessing."

Abram and his nephew Lot begin this journey together. In chapter 13, we discover that Abram and Lot had chosen to separate their clans. Abram settled in Canaan, while Lot moved his tents as far as Sodom. Lot and his family are captured in a battle and Abram must go to his rescue.

Chapter 15 takes up the story after the rescue of Lot. God again speaks to Abram, reminding him of His promises to him. "After these things the word of the LORD came to Abram in a vision, saying, 'Do not fear, Abram, / I am a shield to you; / Your reward shall be very great.'" Abram is perplexed by the promises of the Lord because they are based on his progeny, and he has no children. "And Abram said, 'O Lord GOD, what wilt Thou give me, since I am childless, and the heir of my house is Eliezer of Damascus?'"

The word Adonai is the word translated "Lord." The word translated "God" is the name Yahweh. When Yahweh occurs, it is denoted by the use of LORD, in all capitals. Yet, when Adonai and Yahweh occur together, the English translation "Lord, LORD" would be confusing and therefore most English Bibles employ the translation, "Lord God."

Abram is confused about God's promise to make him a great nation when he is childless still. Abram suggests that Eliezer, his slave, is his only heir, but God assures him that his heir shall come from his own body (15:3–4). The Lord took Abram outside and instructed him to look toward the heavens and count the stars. God then reassures Abram that his descendants will be countless like the stars of the heavens. "Then he believed in the LORD [Yahweh]; and He reckoned it to him as righteousness. And He said to him, 'I am the LORD who brought you out of Ur of the Chaldeans, to give you this land to possess it,' And he said, 'O Lord GOD [Adonai Yahweh], how may I know that I shall possess it?'" (15:6–8).

In this encounter with God, Abram came to a point of surrender where He had to acknowledge his own insufficiency and God's sufficiency. Abram acknowledges that Yahweh is the Lord (Adonai) of his life. However, you should notice that Abram's confession, recorded in verse 2, is immediately followed by an argument that comes from human doubt. Abram asks how this promise could be fulfilled since he is childless. In essence, Abram was in one moment confessing that Yahweh was Lord and then suggesting that the Lord would have trouble fulfilling His own promise.

God's response to Abram is profound. By showing him the stars of the heavens, He declares His authority over all creation. Then God reminds Abram that He had brought him out of Ur of the Chaldeans. In a sense, God is saying to Abram, "Do you think your childlessness presents me with a problem? If you really know who I am, you will have no doubt. Go outside, look up and see the stars. Can you even count the vast number of stars that I have created?" Of course, the answer was "No." Abram had to realize that the God who created those stars could easily bring children to him.

The Dual Meaning of Lordship

What do we mean when we say that Yahweh is Master? I would suggest that lordship has a dual meaning. On the one hand, lordship means complete possession by God. On the other hand, it requires the complete submission of those who would call Him Lord. Thus, when Abram confessed that Yahweh was his Lord, he was recognizing God's sovereign ownership and his own submission. He had declared that God was owner and that Abram was His to command as He desired.

The fact is, many of us struggle with this issue of ownership, don't we? From the very first time we understand what *mine* means, we want to cling to and claim ownership. Take for example two children who are playing together with a toy someone has given to one of them. The children did nothing to deserve the toy. They did not pay for it. Yet as soon as one of the children attempts to play alone with the toy, what happens? The "owner" of the toy snatches it back with a screeching protest, "Mine!"

Somehow, all of us have the mistaken notion that we are owners. We claim that we own a house or a piece of land. We also are aware that ownership brings with it frustrations. Ownership rarely proves to be all we expect it to be. We buy a home only to find that we desire a bigger home or another home in a different location. We also discover that ownership is fraught with the constant demand of repair and maintenance. The roof leaks the week before the plumbing backs up. We can be so frustrated with ownership that we are tempted to say that we were much happier when we owned nothing.

I've got news for you. You can get out of the business of ownership. Truth is, you're not an owner; you're simply a steward. The Lord is owner of all that exists. I have a practical suggestion that will help you acknowledge this. Sit down during your devotional time, take out a piece of paper and make up a deed signing everything over to God, the rightful owner. Say, "Lord, this has never been mine. Somehow I just took over what is yours by creation. I am excited to acknowledge that I am a steward and that you are owner of all the possessions represented on this deed."

One of my deacons in Norfolk shared with me his personal testimony of the freedom he found when he finally understood that the Lord was the owner of everything. A few weeks after he had signed everything over to the Lord, the Lord's washing machine quit working. He told me that in the past such an event would have created frustration and despair. In this instance, he and his wife simply knelt down in front of the washing machine and said, "Lord, Your washing machine has broken down. What do You want to do about it?" After praying and consulting with a repairman, they determined the Lord needed a new washing machine. They could then thank the Lord that He had provided the resources for them to have a washing machine when so many had less. The understanding that the Lord and Master owns everything helps us to keep life in perspective.

Folks, this really is good news. It is a joy to be a steward for the sovereign God of the universe, who has revealed Himself to be holy and righteous. We can rest in the assurance that He is trustworthy and able to provide for our every need. Like Abraham, we will discover that He who has brought us from Ur of the Chaldeans can fulfill His promises in our life. In these days of unprecedented anxiety and fear, we need to discover that God is Adonai.

ADONAI SIGNALS A CALL TO SERVICE

Exodus 4 provides us with another use of the name Adonai that enables us to further understand what it means when we acknowledge God's lordship over our lives. Remember that during the confrontation with God at the burning bush, Moses had discovered God as Yahweh, the self-existent One, who was present to accomplish His will through Moses.

When we rejoin the account in chapter 4, Moses is still trying to explain to his Creator why it would be impossible for him to accomplish his assigned task. Look at verse 10. "Then Moses said to the LORD, 'Please, Lord, I have never been eloquent, neither recently nor in time past, nor since Thou hast spoken to Thy servant; for I am slow of speech and slow of tongue.'" You will notice that the verse contains LORD spelled with all capitals and then with only a capital L. Thus Moses addresses Yahweh as his Adonai, or Lord. What makes the passage a curious contradiction in terms is that Moses addresses God as Lord and acknowledges that he is a servant, but then he attempts to excuse himself from obeying his Lord based on his supposed inability.

Look now at the Lord's response in verses 11 and 12. "And the LORD said to him, 'Who has made man's mouth? Or who makes him dumb or deaf, or seeing or blind? Is it not I, the LORD? Now then go, and I, even I, will be with your mouth, and teach you what you are to say.'" God patiently reminds His servant, Moses, that He is also his Creator who has made him. If God could give man life, He can certainly put words in his mouth.

You would think that God's explanation and promise would have been sufficient to elicit his servant's obedience. Yet we must note Moses' response, recorded in verse 13: "But he said, 'Please, Lord [Adonai], now send the message by whomever Thou wilt.'" The context makes it clear that Moses is not agreeing to go on the mission, but is requesting that God send whomever He will, as long as it is not him. We are told that God's anger burned against Moses for his disobedience. How could the servant dare to argue with the Lord, especially when the Lord is sovereign God, the Creator and Redeemer.

We have already discovered that the name Adonai acknowledges God's ownership of everything. Now we can further conclude that the acknowledgment of lordship requires that we willingly and obediently serve Him. Remember, we were created by God (the truth of Elohim) who is Yahweh, active in history to accomplish His will. When we enter into relationship with Him, we will discover our true purpose in life—to serve and glorify Him. Thus, when we call Him Lord, we must be prepared to serve Him.

Because our Lord is Yahweh, the self-existent, sovereign God of the universe, He has promised to empower us to do whatever He calls us to do. We don't need to be anxious or doubting about whether we are worthy to serve Him or capable of serving Him. The wonderful news is that He has made us worthy and that He desires to work through us to accomplish His purpose on earth. This single truth could transform your life.

DISCOVERING THE JOY OF LORDSHIP

Gideon was one of the great deliverers of Israel. His story, recorded in the sixth chapter of the Book of Judges, begins with an account of how the Midianites were devastating the land where the Israelites were dwelling. In desperation, the people of Israel cried out for deliverance from the hands of the Midianites, and God sent a messenger to Gideon while he was beating out some wheat in a winepress. The angel addressed him as a valiant warrior (6:12). Gideon apparently did not agree with the angel's assessment of his ability and calling, for he demonstrated a great reluctance to be the instrument that God would use in the deliverance of Israel.

Gideon questioned the messenger who had been sent to call him into service. Gideon wanted to know why all the tragedy had come upon their land. Then he asked why they had not seen miracles like those that had been witnessed by their fathers (6:13). In response, Yahweh looked at him and said, "Go in this your strength and deliver Israel from the hand of Midian. Have I not sent you?" (6:14). Gideon's response was immediate. He began to explain to the Lord of the universe why it would be impossible for him to be a deliverer of Israel. "And he said to Him, 'O Lord [Adonai], how shall I deliver Israel? Behold, my family is the least in Manasseh, and I am the youngest in my father's house'" (6:15). God's word of confirmation and assurance was direct but simple. "Surely I will be with you, and you shall defeat Midian as one man" (6:16).

King David loved the name Adonai. As you read the psalms, you will find this name repeated frequently. Perhaps we will discover why this name was so dear to David if we look at 2 Samuel 7, where David expresses his desire to build a house for the ark of God. At first, the prophet Nathan tells him that he may do all that is in his mind. Later, Nathan informs David that God will not allow him to build the temple. Through the prophet, God reminds David that He took him from the pasture to be the ruler over His people Israel and that He has been with him and protected him from his enemies and made him a great name. Then God promises David that He will allow his son to build the temple and that He will establish his kingdom forever.

David's response to this news is one of profound humility. "Then David the king went in and sat before the LORD, and he said, 'Who am I, O Lord GOD [Adonai Yahweh], and what is my house, that Thou hast brought me this far? And yet this was insignificant in Thine eyes, O Lord GOD, for Thou hast spoken also of the house of Thy servant concerning the distant future. And this is the custom of man, O Lord GOD. And again what more can David say to Thee? For Thou knowest Thy servant, O Lord GOD! For the sake of Thy word, and according to Thine own heart, Thou hast done all this greatness to let Thy servant know'" (7:18–21).

Did you notice the repeated references to Yahweh as Lord? David acknowledges his role as servant. He is profoundly moved that the sovereign God of the universe would choose to use such a humble servant. He declares that there is none like God. God has confirmed His word to His servant and empowered him to do whatever He has called him to do. Read the chapter and underline the numerous references to the Lord God. David is moved by the privilege given him to serve His Lord in whatever role he is given to accomplish.

The New Testament is replete with the images of owner-ship and service. Jesus taught His disciples by example and through instruction that greatness in the kingdom is measured in terms of service. In John's Gospel we read these sobering words: "'If anyone serves Me, let him follow Me; and where I am, there shall My servant also be; if anyone serves Me, the

Father will honor him'" (12:26). In the very next chapter of that same Gospel we find the story of Jesus washing the feet of His disciples. After this profound object lesson, Jesus declares: "You call Me Teacher and Lord; and you are right, for so I am. If I then, the Lord and the Teacher, washed your feet, you also ought to wash one another's feet. For I gave you an example that you also should do as I did to you" (13:13–15). To call Jesus Lord we surrender ourselves to His ownership and commit ourselves to serve as He served.

The apostle Paul often referred to himself as a bondslave, which was a slave or servant who had voluntarily placed himself at the disposal of his master. When he writes to his young protégé Timothy, he speaks of Christ as Lord who had put him into service. "I thank Christ Jesus our Lord, who has strengthened me, because He considered me faithful, putting me into service" (1 Tim. 1:12). Notice the unique elements of lordship: Christ places us in service and empowers or strengthens us to accomplish the task.

Three Characteristics of Those Who Know God as Adonai

Throughout the Scriptures, those who know God as Adonai will always exhibit three characteristics:

- They acknowledge themselves as servants. They understand that God is the Owner of all and they are merely stewards who have been declared worthy by Him to serve. They count it a privilege to serve the living God.
- They understand that their Master can supply all their needs, and that He is the One who provides the

supernatural empowerment that enables them to serve God effectively.

- They realize that they can do whatever God calls them to do.

One of my favorite Old Testament stories is found in the Book of Daniel. It concerns a group of young Israelite men who stood for God in a pagan environment. The critical verse that enables us to understand the source of their strength and victory is Daniel 11:32b: "'But the people who know their God will display strength and take action.'" Once we come to fully understand who God is and what He desires to do in our lives, it transforms our willingness to serve and our understanding of the inexhaustible resources available to us.

Whom do you serve? Adonai or yourself? If I looked in your checkbook what evidence would I find about your priorities? Is God Adonai in your life? Is He Adonai in your giving? Is He Adonai in your serving?

Most people demonstrate their confusion about ownership with the simple pronouns they use in everyday conversation. When asked to serve, they say, "I don't have the time," or "My time is valuable." It's not *your* time, it's God's time, and our responsibility is to use it according to His desire. At other times, I hear folks say, "Well I just haven't made up my mind where I will serve." According to 1 Corinthians 12:18, God places us in His service wherever He chooses.

Do you understand that God alone is the Owner, and that you are chosen and empowered by Him to be His steward? Here is a simple definition of stewardship: *Stewardship is the process of managing God's resources according to His plan for His glory.*

APPLYING WHAT WE HAVE LEARNED

Do you believe that there are some Christians who simply can't witness? I've heard people say, "I just can't do that. I would never be able to get the words out." Jesus told His early followers that they were witnesses. The Great Commission was inclusive of all followers of Jesus Christ. In 2 Corinthians 5, Paul declares that we are ambassadors for Christ, as though God were entreating the world through us. And yet, like Moses, we say, "Lord, I can't." Don't you see that it is incompatible to say "Lord" and "I can't"?

Let's try another question. Do you believe there are some circumstances under which you couldn't possibly offer back to God His tithe and your offering? You may be thinking, "You just don't understand my situation. I've got 'mal-tuition.'" That's the dreaded disease that doesn't end until your youngest child reaches graduation. I understand your predicament. I had two daughters in college at one time, with a third one in private school. Yet, we know that the Bible teaches that we need to honor the Lord through our giving. The truth is, God owns everything. The giving of the tithe and offering is simply a means of acknowledging that He is Adonai, and that He alone can supply all our needs according to His riches in glory.

One of the most wonderful breakthroughs in our Christian experience is when we come to understand that God is Adonai. He is Lord of all, and He wants to make His resources available to you so that you may serve Him effectively.

3

E L   E L Y O N

G O D   M O S T   H I G H

"Blessed be Abram of God Most High,

Possessor of heaven and earth;

And blessed be God Most High,

Who has delivered your enemies into your hand."

GENESIS 14:19–20A

The names *El Shaddai* and *El Elyon* have become quite familiar to many Christians because of their use in contemporary music. But what precisely do these names mean? What comfort or encouragement can we derive when we understand that God is El Elyon? The name El Elyon is derived from a combination that begins with the simple word *El.* The term *El,* a general term that expresses majesty and power, is used 238 times in the Old Testament.

Common to the Hebrew, Aramaic, and Arabic languages, El was frequently used as a reference to deity in many of the nations surrounding Israel during biblical times. For example, El was the name of one of the high gods of the Canaanites. In Exodus 34:14, God says, "For you shall not worship any other god [el], for the LORD [Yahweh], whose name is Jealous, is a jealous God." In Deuteronomy 3:24, we find another use of El to refer to deity in general: "'"O Lord GOD [Adonai Jehovah], Thou hast begun to show Thy servant Thy greatness and Thy strong hand; for what god [el] is there in heaven or on earth who can do such works and mighty acts as Thine?"'" The God of Israel stands apart from all the supposed gods of other nations in that He reveals Himself in human history by His deeds. We will not focus on the singular name El, but on the compound El Elyon, which means "God Most High."

As we look at the various names by which God has revealed Himself, remember that God is One and He alone is God. The Jewish affirmation of the unity and uniqueness of God is called the Shema. "'Hear, O Israel! The LORD is our God, the LORD is one! And you shall love the LORD your God with all your heart and with all your soul and with all your might'" (Deut. 6:4–5). God's various names reveal His multifaceted character. It is like viewing a diamond. As we turn the stone in our hand, we see

different facets of its beauty revealed as light is refracted into prisms of color. In like manner, God's many names reveal unique aspects of His nature and character.

THE HISTORICAL CONTEXT OF EL ELYON

In order to adequately understand the name El Elyon, we must study it in its historical context. The name is first used of God in Genesis 14, after Lot had determined to separate his people and livestock from Abram. Lot chose the lush land of the Jordan valley by sight, settling in the plains near the Dead Sea and moving his tents as far as Sodom (13:12). He chose impetuously what appeared to be a fertile valley, without regard to God's purposes or the potential impact of sin. Abram, by faith, moved to the oaks of Mamre, which are in Hebron, whereupon his first action was to build an altar and worship the Lord.

If we are not careful, we may find ourselves, like Lot, making decisions based on sight rather than faith. We make choices that are dictated by the world's standards of value and success. Sometimes we make decisions about our career based on the promise of financial reward, without regard for the consequences that decision may bring on our family.

It is always an encouragement when we see someone move by faith in obedience to God. Take, for example, Dr. Rebekah Naylor, an eminent surgeon and the daughter of Dr. Robert Naylor, the fifth president of Southwestern Baptist Theological Seminary. How do you explain her choice to devote her career to the people of Banglor, India? No doubt she passed up a financially prosperous career as a surgeon here in the United States to serve in virtual obscurity in India. Yet, by faith and in obedience to God, she determined to move to the place where God

assigned her. Like Abraham, she discovered that God is El Elyon, God Most High.

Let's finish the story of how Abraham came to understand that God was El Elyon. Lot's triumph and joy in Sodom was short-lived. Not only were the people of Sodom intensely wicked, but the whole area was politically unstable. There were many small cities ruled by kings with limited resources. Periodically, a stronger king would overthrow a weaker king and annex the defeated city to create more power for himself. From time to time, those who had been conquered would rebel to reestablish their freedom. This political instability would frequently boil over into war.

One of the chief characters in our story is Chedorlaomer, king of Elam. Chedorlaomer headed a coalition of Mesopotamian states, and the kings of Sodom, Gomorrah, and three other neighboring city-states had been paying tribute to him for nearly twelve years. In the thirteenth year, the five kings rebelled, asserting their independence (Gen. 14:4). Chedorlaomer seized the opportunity of their rebellion to gather his allies and extend his kingdom. A battle was fought in the valley of Siddim (the Dead Sea area) and many people died. The survivors fled to the hill country (14:10).

Thus the attempted rebellion of these five city-states was quickly put down and the story may have been little more than a blip on the historical timeline of the area, if not for one small factor. Genesis 14:11 tells us that the victors took all the goods of Sodom and Gomorrah and all their food supply and departed. But that's not all they took! "And they also took Lot, Abram's nephew, and his possessions and departed, for he was living in Sodom" (14:12).

Uncle Abram to the Rescue

A fugitive of the battle survived and brought Abram the news of his nephew's capture. Because Lot still lived in a covenant relationship with his uncle, when Abram heard that Lot had been taken captive, he marshaled his own forces and pursued the enemy as far as Dan, where he strategically divided his forces at night and accomplished total victory. Genesis 14:16 gives us a glimpse of this conquest. "And he brought back all the goods, and also brought back his relative Lot with his possessions, and also the women, and the people."

In spite of Lot's foolish choice and rebellious spirit, Abram was empowered by God to bring him out of captivity. The victory did not simply release Lot; it liberated all the people and possessions that had been taken by Chedorlaomer and his allies.

A Deal He Could Refuse

What occurs next creates a fascinating backdrop against which God reveals Himself as El Elyon. As Abram returned from battle, he was met by two kings, the king of Sodom and a king named Melchizedek. The first to go out to meet Abram was the king of Sodom (Gen. 14:17), a defected ruler whose army had fled to the hill country to survive Chedorlaomer's attack. The king of Sodom was at Abram's mercy because Abram had defeated his conquerors. You might expect that the king of Sodom would have knelt before Abram, hailing him as deliverer, but instead he represents all that Sodom stood for—sinful disobedience, worldly pleasure, and self-confidence.

With his self-confidence remarkably intact, the king of Sodom makes an offer: "Give the people to me and take the goods for yourself" (14:21). Can you believe his audacity? He offered Abram the captured goods if he would return his people, ignoring the fact that Abram had the right to keep *everything*. Abram was the victor. The king of Sodom had no bargaining rights; he had no chips on the table, yet he tried to strike a deal.

It is typical of fallen man to want to negotiate when he has nothing of value to offer. I frequently share the gospel with people who feel that they can bargain with God about their entry into heaven. They contend that they are not bad people or that they are better than most Christians they have met. They argue about the good deeds they have accomplished. Occasionally I meet Christians who are trying to strike a deal with God about areas of compromise or disobedience. We sound like the king of Sodom, demanding our rights, trying to strike a deal with God. Until we fully recognize God's sufficiency, and our insufficiency, we will never know Him as El Elyon.

Look at Abram's response to the king of Sodom. "And Abram said to the king of Sodom, 'I have sworn to the LORD God Most High [El Elyon], possessor of heaven and earth, that I will not take a thread or a sandal thong or anything that is yours, lest you should say, "I have made Abram rich"'" (14:22–23). Abram refused to take anything other than what his men had eaten. He refused even a thread or a shoestring. He didn't want the king of Sodom, the king of self-sufficiency, to take credit. Abram had already discovered that God Most High is the owner of everything. He refused to look for resources for victory from anyone else.

Though Genesis 14:22 is an important reference to El Elyon, it is not the first time that name appears in the Bible. For the initial reference, we must look back four verses to Genesis 14:18, where Abram meets Melchizedek, king of Salem.

The Priest of El Elyon

The contrast between the two kings could not be more striking. The king of Sodom, with nothing to offer, came to meet Abram, asking for his people. Melchizedek comes with provisions: "And Melchizedek king of Salem brought out bread and wine; now he was a priest of God Most High [El Elyon]. And he blessed him and said, 'Blessed be Abram of God Most High [El Elyon], / Possessor of heaven and earth; / And blessed be God Most High, / Who has delivered your enemies into your hand'" (14:18–20). Three times in this short passage we encounter the name El Elyon.

Melchizedek provided sustenance for Abram and blessed him in the name of El Elyon, "God Most High." Apparently it was a common name for divinity throughout the country of Palestine at this time. What is distinctive in this context is that El Elyon is identified as the possessor of heaven and earth and is further identified by Abram as Yahweh. Notice the use of LORD in verse 22 in relationship with El Elyon.

The context makes it clear that it was El Elyon who had delivered Abram and not his own military genius or the supply of any earthly king. Thus the king of Salem greets Abram with a blessing acknowledging that it was God Most High who had delivered the enemy into Abram's hand. Look again at the progression of events. First the king of Sodom greets Abram. Then the king of Salem, which means "peace" and is to be identified with Jerusalem, greets him with provision and a blessing, recognizing the true source of Abram's victory. Then the king of Sodom offers a deal that the patriarch keep all the spoils but give him back his servants.

Abram's response to the two kings is as strong a contrast as the two kings are themselves. He tells the king of Sodom that he has sworn to the Lord God Most High that he will take nothing from the hand of the king of Sodom, lest he then take any credit for the blessing that has come to Abram's life. Yet in response to the king of Salem, Abram gave him a tenth of all he had captured (Gen. 14:20). He spontaneously gave a tithe to the king (who was also priest) as an expression of gratitude both to God and His servant, Melchizedek.

It is instructive to note that the concept of the tithe as a spontaneous expression of gratitude was practiced well before the giving of the law. It is thus surprising that some Christians want to argue that tithing is legalistic and thus should be jettisoned under the doctrine of grace.

Melchizedek, king of Salem and priest of El Elyon, makes a somewhat mysterious appearance in this story. We can't fail to note King David's mention of him in Psalm 110, where the psalmist refers to this king and priest of Salem (later Jerusalem) as he anticipates a greater Melchizedek yet to come. The psalm begins:

> The LORD says to my Lord:
> "Sit at My right hand,
> Until I make Thine enemies a
>   footstool for Thy feet." (v. 1)

The first use of LORD here translates the word Yahweh, and the second mention of Lord is Adonai. In the New Testament, in Acts 2:34–35, Luke tells us that Peter quotes Psalm 110:1 to demonstrate that Jesus was the long-awaited Messiah. Peter's argument is that the prophetic words of David could have referred to no one other than Jesus Himself. Note further in Psalm 110:4 that the Messiah will be a priest forever after the order of Melchizedek:

> The LORD [Yahweh] has sworn and will not
>   change His mind,
> "Thou art a priest forever
> According to the order of Melchizedek."

The author of Hebrews draws our attention yet again to Melchizedek. In chapter 7, he recounts the story of Abraham's encounter with Melchizedek and then quotes the promise in Psalm 110:4. Let's look at the first few verses: "For this Melchizedek, king of Salem, priest of the Most High God, who met Abraham as he was returning from the slaughter of the kings and blessed him, to whom also Abraham apportioned a tenth part of all the spoils, was first of all, by the translation of his name, king of righteousness, and then also king of Salem, which is king of peace. Without father, without mother, without genealogy, having neither beginning of days nor end of life, but made like the Son of God, he abides a priest perpetually" (Heb. 7:1–3). The author of Hebrews draws a parallel between Jesus and Melchizedek to argue that Jesus was a priest after the order of Melchizedek, rather than the order of Aaron. The emphasis in chapter 7 is on righteousness, peace, and personal worth, by which Christ was proclaimed a perpetual high priest. The Son of God, because He is eternal, could be in reality what Melchizedek could only be as a type. Thus, if Abraham would bring tithes to an earthly king, Melchizedek, how much more should we present our tithes to the heavenly King, Jesus?

THE SIGNIFICANCE OF THE NAME EL ELYON

The key to understanding the name El Elyon is to note its identification with Yahweh and with the affirmation that He is the

Possessor of heaven and earth. Thus it naturally follows that only He could have given Abram the victory over His enemies, for He alone is God.

It is interesting to note that the name El Elyon is used repeatedly in the Book of Daniel, where the author recounts some of the events that occurred when Israel languished in Babylonian captivity. In both Genesis and in Daniel, we should note that there is a faith claim that moves beyond the boundaries of the nation of Israel. God is thus seen as universal in His reign and rule. The nations surrounding Israel were polytheistic in their worship. Thus the revelation of this name and its identification with Yahweh declares that God alone is God. Jehovah is Creator and Provider, He is God Most High. To put it simply, He is God alone.

In the Book of Acts, we encounter the story of the apostle Paul in Athens. As he walked through the city, he saw idols everywhere and observed an altar to an unknown god. He used that discovery as a beginning point for his message to the Athenians. He noted that they were a religious people. "'For while I was passing through and examining the objects of your worship, I also found an altar with this inscription, "TO AN UNKNOWN GOD." What therefore you worship in ignorance, this I proclaim to you'" (Acts 17:23). Further, Paul declared that the Lord God is He, the God who created everything and is Lord of heaven and earth. He is the one who made from one every nation of mankind and appointed their time and boundaries.

Paul did not use the name El Elyon, but his message to the Athenians bears the same impact that the use of that name bears in Genesis 14 and in Daniel. It declares that while people may worship gods they make with their hands or call by various names, there is only one God in all the earth and He is the Creator of all that is. The God of Israel (Yahweh) is the Creator and Ruler of all the earth. He alone is a personal and living and knowable God.

THREE PRINCIPLES TO LEARN

What does this biblical history mean to us at the beginning of the twenty-first century? It is a wonderful story, but isn't it simply a historical footnote that belongs to Israel's tradition? I would suggest that it has three profound implications for us today.

First, it creates a mandate for evangelism because we learn that all other "supposed gods" are false gods. One of the reasons that persons truly committed to Christ are often assertive in telling others about Jesus is because the Bible makes it clear that God alone is God and that His Son is the only One who can provide access to God.

At my first church, I sat one day over lunch with a prominent businessman who was also a member of our church. Although he did not attend with great frequency, he indicated that he had been following my progress at the church and was quite pleased in most respects. He didn't, however, appreciate my strong emphasis on evangelism. Although he claimed to be a Christian, he didn't feel it was necessary to tell others about Christ, because, he said, all paths ultimately led to God. He suggested that as long as one was sincere about one's belief, it was sufficient. This avowed Christian was in actuality a universalist, arguing that everyone would ultimately be saved by the sincerity of their belief.

I replied that I couldn't agree, because the Scriptures, which had revealed Christ to us, also declared that there was only one true God, who created the heavens and the earth. He thus had the right to be worshiped by His created beings and He alone could provide the way for sinful man to have access to Him. This he accomplished by the incredible gift of His Son, who paid the penalty for man's sin.

This truth demands that we declare Him to the nations. This is why the Great Commission in Matthew 28:19–20 insists that we make disciples of all people on the earth. It is a tragedy that many who claim Christ have not studied the Bible sufficiently to understand that if the claims of Christ are true, then any other claim to know God outside of Christ must be false. A further tragedy is that many Christians who would agree with my conclusions to this point live their Christian lives like functional universalists. Their failure to share the good news of the Bible with their unsaved friends implies that they must believe their neighbors' unbelief or false belief to be sufficient.

The understanding that God is the Possessor of the heavens and the earth gives a basis for our faith in the midst of crisis. This name, Most High God, grounds our faith in the greatest miracle of all time, the creation of the world. The point is that we are not self-made; the power of life has been given to us by the Creator of the world. Abram refused the gifts of the king of Sodom because he understood that Sodom had no power to provide him with any sustenance.

Many Christians say they can trust God for their eternal security, yet they struggle to trust Him to provide the resources for daily living. When we find ourselves in a crisis, we are tempted to think that our old self-reliance (Sodom) can provide the resources of life. We attempt to live the victorious Christian life in our own strength and we fail.

If God can make the heavens and the earth, He can provide the necessities of life. Why do we struggle when we choose a life mate? Why do we struggle to trust Him with our children when they are away at college? Why do we struggle to trust Him with our finances? The God of creation can provide all the resources to enable us to live victoriously.

You may find it interesting that the psalmist frequently assures his readers that God can meet their everyday needs, based on the fact that He is the Maker of the heaven and the earth.

- Psalm 115:15: "May you be blessed of the LORD, / Maker of heaven and earth."
- Psalm 121:2: "My help comes from the LORD, / Who made heaven and earth."
- Psalm 124:8: "Our help is in the name of the LORD, / Who made heaven and earth."
- Psalm 134:3: "May the LORD bless you from Zion, / He who made heaven and earth."

Notice that, in each of these references, the focus is on the power of the Creator to bring you help in the midst of daily circumstances. When you understand the truth that your God is El Elyon, like Abram you can refuse to take anything from the hand of the king of Sodom. You do not need to be self-sufficient; you need to be God-sufficient.

The understanding of God's sovereign care should come to govern all of life. When Abram recognized that the resources for his victory came from God alone, he responded by giving a tenth of the spoils to Melchizedek. Thus Abram's understanding of God's provision impacted both his living and his giving. You may be thinking that I'm making an appeal for tithing. In truth, I think Christians should joyously give beyond the tithe out of their gratitude to God for His constant provision. Further, it reveals that we trust Him to provide for our needs tomorrow. Tithing is a God-given opportunity to demonstrate that you trust God with the very sustenance of life.

The anxious, selfish lifestyle of our nation portrays our self-sufficiency, our dependence on the king of Sodom. It demonstrates a lack of understanding of the true Source of all resources. If you want to live above anxiety, rest in the truth that God is the sovereign King of the universe. Your needs will never be met by the world, but they can be fully met by El Elyon.

4

EL SHADDAI

ALMIGHTY GOD

Now when Abram was ninety-nine years old,
the LORD appeared to Abram and said to him,
"I am God Almighty; Walk before Me
and be blameless."

GENESIS 17:1

What will it take to make you truly happy? What will it take to relieve the anxiety you feel? When do you think you might reach that state of contentment? Is it possible?

Our first response to such queries is often in financial terms. When I have enough to pay all my bills and have some left over. When I have enough put aside to retire comfortably. But I have discovered a curious fact; no one seems to know how much is enough for contentment.

A pivotal event in my early pastoral ministry in Norfolk, Virginia, helped to solidify my own thinking concerning such matters. Our church was experiencing incredible growth, which had created numerous challenges. One such challenge was parking space. We didn't have any.

Our church membership consisted mainly of hard-working, low- to middle-income families. They gave freely of what they had, but our budget was inadequate to meet the growing needs of our church. At that time we had only one man in the church membership who might have been considered wealthy. He had acquired extensive property in Virginia Beach before it became a popular resort area. As the land escalated in value, he had sold off his holdings quite profitably.

We were trying to raise money for a small parking lot. We needed $60,000 for a lot that would hold sixty cars. A lot this size wouldn't begin to meet our needs, but raising even $60,000 was a stretch. To keep the church aware of our progress, we designed a board showing the parking lot and we sold little cars for $1000 each to place on the board. Few of our people could purchase an entire car and thus small sections of the cars were often displayed.

I knew this gentleman could purchase ten or fifteen of those cars without even giving it a second thought. Such a gift would have given us an incredible boost toward reaching our goal. As I walked this retired businessman across the site of the proposed parking lot, I asked him if he would consider getting us started by buying ten spaces.

He looked at me and acknowledged that he had experienced wonderful years of prosperity. The economy in Virginia Beach had been good. Then he told me that no one knew how long the good economy would hold up and therefore he had to protect his assets. Then he added a postscript: "Pastor, I'm facing an additional tax bill for nearly $50,000 this year. You wouldn't understand what it is like to be in that income bracket."

I knew that he was right about that. I would probably never know what it was like to be in an income bracket that required an additional $50,000 in taxes. I will never forget the fear he had about the future, his uncertainty about the sufficiency of his resources.

How much is enough? That question will never be answered in terms of money. It can only be answered when we come to realize that God is enough. Have you come to the point in your personal relationship with God that He is enough? Is He sufficient to meet all your needs? Can He be trusted to fulfill the promises of His Word? For example, the Bible tells us that we can do all things through Christ who strengthens us. Have you found that to be true in your own life? The Bible commands us to be anxious for nothing. How many of us live without anxiety? Are these promises just another form of whistling in the dark? Do we recite these promises without letting them transform our lives?

Abram faced a faith crisis event that God used to show him that He was sufficient to fulfill His promises. You remember that God had promised to make Abram the father of a mighty nation. There was, however, one small problem. Abram was ninety-nine years old and childless.

ABRAM'S NEED AND GOD'S PROMISE

The name *El Shaddai* occurs for the first time in Genesis 17. To understand the import of this name fully, we must begin in Genesis 12, where God gave Abram a commission fortified with a promise. God called Abram to leave his country and his relatives and to inhabit a land which He would show him. It took a great leap of faith for Abram to leave all that was familiar to him for a land that was presently occupied by others. But Abram's faith was fortified with a powerful promise:

> "And I will make you a great nation,
> And I will bless you,
> And make your name great;
> And so you shall be a blessing." (Gen. 12:2)

God's promise is made more explicit in Genesis 13:16. "'And I will make your descendants as the dust of the earth; so that if anyone can number the dust of the earth, then your descendants can also be numbered.'"

As the drama unfolds, we are constantly reminded of Abram's childless state. In the previous chapter, we studied the name El Elyon. Abram came to understand that Yahweh was also God Most High, the possessor of heaven and earth (Gen. 14:19). Now, in Genesis 15, we are told that after Abram had rescued Lot the Lord spoke to Abram in a vision: "'Do not fear, Abram, / I am a shield to you; / Your reward shall be very great'" (15:1).

Abram's frustration bubbles to the surface as he responds, "O Lord God, what wilt Thou give me, since I am childless, and the heir of my house is Eliezer of Damascus?" (15:2).

The suggestion that Eliezer would be the heir of his house is a subtle attempt on the part of Abram to help God out of a jam. Here is a promise of God that appears to have no chance of being fulfilled. Abram is aging and he has no natural heir. There may even be a note of reproach in his response to God: "Since Thou hast given no offspring to me, one born in my house is my heir" (15:3). Immediately, God confirms His promise to Abram. Eliezer is not to be his heir but a child that will come from his own body. God then gives Abram a little object lesson in faith. "And He took him outside and said, 'Now look toward the heavens, and count the stars, if you are able to count them.' And He said to him, 'So shall your descendants be'" (15:5). The text tells us very simply that Abram believed God's promise and it was reckoned to him as righteousness.

As we continue on the journey of faith with Abram and Sarai, we are again reminded of their condition. "Now Sarai, Abram's wife had borne him no children . . ." (Gen. 16:1). After a lifetime of barrenness, Sarai now becomes desperate and convinces Abram to go in to her Egyptian maid, Hagar. This fleshly act to help God fulfill His promise created disastrous results. When Hagar conceived, Sarai despised her and treated her harshly. Hagar fled from Sarai's presence, but an angel of the Lord convinced her to return and submit herself to Sarai. Out of Abram's union with Hagar was born the child Ishmael.

Up to this point in the drama, the promise of God remains unfulfilled and the situation seems only to have worsened. But before we become too judgmental about the actions of Abram and Sarai, perhaps we need to take stock of the times in our own lives when we have struggled with the promises of God and have attempted to help Him out through our own resources. All of us wrestle with maintaining an absolute faith response to God. We trust God fully and totally for forgiveness and salvation, but then we live the Christian life as though everything depended on us. We may even piously quote the apocryphal verse, "God helps those who help themselves!"

In the New Testament, Paul cautions the Galatian church about the tendency to begin the Christian journey by faith and then attempt to live it by the power of the flesh. "This is the only thing I want to find out from you: did you receive the Spirit by the works of the Law, or by hearing with faith? Are you so foolish? Having begun by the Spirit, are you now being perfected by the flesh?" (Gal. 3:2–3).

Faith does not mean a passive resignation. Some people misunderstand this point. I once was involved in a marriage counseling situation where the husband had been without work for a time. When asked about this problem, he responded, "If God wants me to have a job, He will give it to me." The problem, however, revolved around the fact that the husband had neither looked for nor applied for any job openings. His was not a statement of faith, but of passive resignation.

PRACTICING POSITIVE SURRENDER

What was involved in Abram's pilgrimage, and in ours, is a positive and active surrender to the promise of God. We begin chapter 17 of Genesis with the reminder that Abram was ninety-nine years old. By human reckoning, he and Sarai were past childbearing age and thus the promise of God looked like an impossibility. What Abram was to discover was that with God nothing is impossible. When we surrender our will to His, He brings to fulfillment His promises through His power.

It is at this point that God assures Abram by the revelation of the name, El Shaddai, God Almighty. "Now when Abram was ninety-nine years old, the LORD appeared to Abram and said to him, 'I am God Almighty [El Shaddai]; / Walk before Me, and be blameless. / And I will establish My covenant between Me and you, / And I will multiply you exceedingly'" (Gen. 17:1–2). Abram prostrated himself before the Lord in absolute surrender.

With Abram on his face before God, God reminded him of the covenant promise He had made. He again underlines the truth that Abram was to be the father of a multitude of nations. As a sign of this covenant, God changed Abram's name to Abraham. *Abram* meant "exalted father." No doubt that name had been a bitter reminder of the truth that he had fathered no children. The name *Abraham* means "father of a multitude." Sarai's name, which meant "to persist, exert oneself, or contend," was also changed, to *Sarah,* which means "princess." Sarai had exerted herself in coming up with the solution to send Abram in to her handmaiden. Now she would be Sarah, the princess and mother of nations. Abraham was still staggered by the enormity of the promise which God had just confirmed, but he surrendered himself to the will of God.

E L   S H A D D A I :   G O D   A L M I G H T Y

What is the meaning of the name El Shaddai? What new facet of the character of God does it reveal? The name is generally translated as "God Almighty" or "Almighty God." The word *almighty* points to the omnipotence of God; namely, that He is all powerful and able to do anything and everything at any given time.

Yet, is that all that this name intends to convey? It is possible that El Shaddai simply underscores the emphasis of El, conveying the idea of majesty or omnipotence and focusing on the absolute power of God. Yet I think it is likely that *Shaddai* might have a slightly different connotation in this context. Shaddai may be derived from the Hebrew word *shad*, which can be translated as "breast." In this case, the term Shaddai could signify the one who nourishes or supplies. Thus when it is linked with El, it would mean, "the one mighty to nourish" or "the one mighty to supply." This interpretation would thus suggest that God is the One able to pour out His blessings in full abundance.

Let's look together at several significant passages that could help to fortify this translation. In Genesis 49:24–25, we find the story of Jacob blessing his sons and telling them about their future. In regard to Joseph he states:

> "And his arms were agile . . .
> From the God [El] of your father who helps you,
> And by the Almighty [Shaddai] who blesses you
> With blessings of heaven above,
> Blessings of the deep that lies beneath,
> Blessings of the breasts and of the womb."

Notice that it is El who gives strength to the arms, and God as Shaddai who brings the bountiful blessings of the breast and the womb.

Next, we should look at Isaiah 66:10–13, one of the most powerful passages in the Old Testament concerning Israel's restoration. The images of the breast and the womb are found throughout this passage. The prophet calls everyone who loves Jerusalem to be joyful and exceedingly glad, "That you may nurse and be satisfied with her comforting breasts, / That you may suck and be delighted with her bountiful bosom." In verse 12, the prophet declares, "And you shall be nursed, you shall be carried on the hip and fondled on the knees." In verse 13, he likens God's comfort to that of a mother. The word translated "breast" in this passage is *shad*.[1]

Many of the idols of the pagans depict a multibreasted woman. The Egyptian goddess Isis was clustered with breasts. These idols were believed to be responsible for the rain that gave the earth its bounty, yet these stone carvings with their many breasts could supply nothing. In stark contrast, God, who revealed Himself as El Shaddai, is the Almighty One who could bring fruit to an empty womb. He is the living God who could supply in abundance every need. He is the God of comfort who tenderly meets the needs of His people.

Can you imagine the joy Abram must have experienced when he discovered that the God of his heritage was almighty to nourish? He was the only God who could fill the barren womb of Sarai and turn a contender into a princess. If we return to Genesis 17, we will discover that there is a requirement placed on Abram. He must walk before God and be blameless (17:1). God desires to accomplish His purpose through those who have a posture of positive surrender.

A NAME FULFILLED IN CHRIST

El Shaddai, this great name of God which speaks of His inexhaustible riches, was fulfilled in the person of Christ. Do you remember the Lord's encounter with the woman at the well, recorded in John 4? She was laboring to draw water from the deep well. Jesus told her that if she had known who He was, she would have asked for water from Him. Her initial response concerned her physical need for water, but Jesus' concern went much deeper. She was an immoral woman who had struggled from relationship to relationship without finding any contentment. Jesus offered her a spiritual water that would quench the deep thirsting of her soul.

As we read further in John's Gospel (ch. 6), we find the story of the feeding of the multitude from the five loaves and the two fishes, which seemed an impossible task. Yet, when the meal was finished, the disciples picked up twelve baskets full of leftover fragments. Jesus provided for their physical needs with an overflowing abundance.

Later, when the people again seek out Jesus, he observes that the only reason they have followed Him was because they had eaten of the loaves and been filled. When the people reminded Jesus that Moses had fed them with manna in the wilderness, Jesus replies, "Truly, truly, I say to you, it is not Moses who has given you the bread out of heaven, but it is My Father who gives you the true bread out of heaven" (John 6:32). When the people then request that Jesus continually feed them with this heavenly bread, He says, "I am the bread of life; he who comes to Me shall not hunger, and he who believes in Me shall never thirst" (6:35).

Jesus brings to us the inexhaustible riches of God. He provides the water and the bread of life. If you would know God as El Shaddai, you must have a personal relationship with Jesus Christ.

LESSONS FOR TODAY

What lessons can we take from these stories? You may not be faced with the same sort of faith dilemma that confronted Abram, but all of us are faced with faith challenges today.

Lesson one is that salvation can never come by the works of human flesh. There was nothing that Abraham and Sarah could do in their own strength to fulfill the promise of God in their lives. Sadly, I continually encounter people who are trusting in their good works, their church membership, or their acts of kindness to make them right with God.

One of the more sorrowful events in my early ministry occurred in Wolf Creek, Kentucky, where I witnessed to an elderly man whose children attended our church. They knew that their dad was lost and they wanted me to witness to him before he died. After I shared the gospel, he responded that when he got things straightened out in his life, he fully intended to come to God and join the church. I told him that he would never get his life straightened out until he came to know Christ as Savior. If he could save himself, the sacrifice of Christ on the cross would have been unnecessary. Still, he wouldn't commit his life to Christ that day, and it wasn't long before he stepped out of this life into a Christless eternity.

The second lesson is a warning to Christians that they can accomplish nothing for God as long as they think they can do it in their own strength. Many Christians get caught up in an "Avis" brand of Christianity. They just keep "trying harder" to please God. We try to break old habits that continue to plague our Christian lives. We are certain that if we exercise greater willpower, we will achieve a breakthrough. Yet the harder we try, the more frustrated we become. Ultimately, we come to the end of our rope and cry, "I've tried everything else; I think I'll pray." Let me suggest that we need to start on that end of the rope. We need to *begin* in prayer. Once we understand that we can do nothing in ourselves to accomplish God's will, it will radically transform our prayer lives.

If we are going to experience God's fullness, we must empty ourselves. Abraham had to come to the end of his own strategies to provide an heir before he could receive God's promised heir. When you come to the end of your own resources, you will discover that God is sufficient to supply all of your needs according to His riches.

Paula and I learned to depend on God's sufficiency in a graphic way while we were in Cambridge, England. We had stored what little furniture we had, borrowed all the money we could scrape together, and left for three years of study. As we came closer to graduation, the tensions began to mount. Not only was I concerned about the successful completion of my program; I was concerned about providing for my family when I returned to the United States. Additional financial strain was added by the news that Paula was pregnant with our second child, and Kristina was only a year old at the time.

During the spring before my dissertation was due in the fall, I began to talk to a seminary in the U.S. about the possibility of a one-year teaching post in Greek. My ministry goal was to pastor a local church, but I told the dean that I would consider a one-year teaching assignment. As our long-distance correspondence continued, I began to realize that this job would provide necessary financial assistance at a critical time. Further, it would allow me to get back to the U.S., where I could more readily talk to pulpit search committees. I had discovered that few committees would fly to Cambridge to interview a prospective pastor. The seminary job began to look better and better.

One of the faculty members from this particular seminary happened to be on sabbatical in Cambridge at the time. As I discussed with him my goal to eventually pastor a church, he advised me that I should leave my call with the seminary open-ended. He reasoned that they would be less likely to offer me the job if they knew that I was only willing to stay one year. His counsel seemed sound and I had already begun to desire the job for the security it offered my young family. At times, I could even see myself remaining there and becoming a well-respected professor.

The next time I talked with the dean, I told him that while I understood we were discussing a one-year position, I would be willing to stay longer if that was the Lord's will. What I didn't know was that my statement would send a shock wave through the system. You see, the dean had hired other faculty members who had finished all their course work and lacked only the final submission of their dissertations. Some of those professors had never completed their work and thus had created a difficult situation for the dean. Accreditation agencies like to see faculty members with their terminal degrees.

I was expecting my contract in the mail any day. One particular Saturday, the long-awaited letter arrived. Saturdays were special days for Paula and me. We generally slept in a little later than during the week. After I got up, I would get the mail and bring Paula a cup of coffee in bed. After getting the mail this day, I walked dramatically into the bedroom, tossed the letter on the bed and said to Paula, "Read it and weep." She did, on both counts! The dean had decided to offer the job to one of his own graduate students.

I was shell-shocked. How would we get back to the United States? Where would I work? Without a job, how could I provide for a wife and two children? It was during this struggle that we came to realize that God is El Shaddai; He is God Almighty, able to nourish and supply. I also began to realize that I had come to depend on the job offer at the seminary for my sufficiency. In my pride, I had begun to think about the glory of being a popular professor. As we surrendered our will to His, He provided our every need. We had a sense of peace about the direction of the future. Within a few weeks, I had a job offer to teach at Wingate College, a small Baptist school in North Carolina. It was equidistant from both of our parents, which enabled them to help us with the new baby. I can only wonder how different our life might have been if I had taken a job simply for the potential security. I thank God that I now know Him as El Shaddai.

A third lesson we can learn from the story of Abraham is that God has abundant resources to supply all of our needs. Abraham's and Sarah's attempts to help God fulfill His promise pales into insignificance when we see all that God wanted to supply out of His abundance. Too many Christians live impoverished Christian lives even though we have unlimited resources available to us to accomplish God's will. In Ephesians 1, Paul prays that his readers might come to understand the riches of God and the surpassing greatness of His power (vv. 18–19). He then reminds them that God had already placed everything under Christ's feet and established Him as head over the church that it might express His fulness. He then promises them that God is able to do exceedingly, abundantly beyond all that they might ask or think, which He accomplishes according to His power at work in us (Eph. 3:20–21). In the Philippian letter, Paul declares: "I can do all things through Him who strengthens me" (4:13).

We need to discover the truth that God is Almighty to nourish and supply. We have unlimited potential to serve Him effectively.

Finally, we must learn to wait upon God to fulfill His promises in His own time. Abram and Sarai were so eager to see the fulfillment of God's promise of an heir that they continually ran ahead of God. When they did, they began to operate in the flesh and the consequences proved to be disastrous. You will recall the sorrow and tragedy that accompanied the birth of Ishmael. What in your life looks impossible? Have you surrendered it fully to the Lord? Are you willing to wait upon Him to fulfill His promises?

1. In this section I have depended greatly on the discussion of this name by Nathan Stone in his book *Names of God* (Chicago: Moody Press, 1944).

— 5 —

YAHWEH

COVENANTAL GOD

And God said to Moses,

"I AM WHO I AM"; and He said,

"Thus you shall say to the sons of Israel,

'I AM has sent me to you.'"

Exodus 3:14

Does God have a proper name? The psalmist in Psalm 68:4 says:

> Sing to God, sing praises to His name;
> Lift up {a song} for Him who rides through the
>   deserts,
> Whose name is the Lord [Yahweh] and exult
>   before Him.

The prophet Isaiah records this declaration by the Lord:

> "I am the LORD, that is My name;
> I will not give My glory to another,
> Nor My praise to graven images." (42:8)

Most Bible scholars would agree that the name *Yahweh,* or *Jehovah,* as it is sometimes translated, would be the proper name of God. The other names, including the compound names, provide further revelation of His character and His activity.

Jehovah, or Yahweh, occurs 6,823 times in the Bible. Many English translations will translate this name with the word LORD, in all capitals, to distinguish it from Adonai, which is often translated with the word Lord in upper and lowercase letters.

In Hebrew, Yahweh is written with only the four consonants YHWH and no vowels. The Hebrews considered this name so holy that they would not pronounce it for fear that they would profane the holiness of the name. When they came to YHWH in the text, they would substitute the name Adonai. When the Jewish scholars, called Masoretes, added vowel signs sometime before the tenth century A.D., the vowels from the name Adonai were put together with the letters YHWH (translated as JHVH in German) to create the name Jehovah that we find often in our English text.

The Meaning of Yahweh

The first appearance of this name is in Genesis 2:4. Here it is used in combination with the name Elohim. "This is the account of the heavens and the earth when they were created, in the day that the LORD God [Yahweh Elohim] made earth and heaven." This name is used a second time in Genesis 28:13, where we have the account of Jacob's dream at Bethel. "And behold, the LORD stood above it and said, 'I am the LORD [Yahweh], the God [Elohim] of your father Abraham and the God of Isaac; the land on which you lie, I will give it to you and to your descendants.'" In these two contexts we can affirm that Yahweh and Elohim both refer to the one God of the Bible.

The Bible clearly teaches that there is only one true God in the heavens and the earth. We refer to this as the teaching of monotheism, one God. Thus, while we may look at the different names applied to God, we need to clearly understand that God is One and beside Him no other god exists. The prophet Isaiah, recording the words of the Lord, makes this abundantly clear:

> "You are My witnesses," declares the LORD,
> "And My servant whom I have chosen,
> In order that you may know and believe Me,
> And understand that I am He.
> Before Me there was no God formed
> And there will be none after Me." (43:10)

What then is the meaning or significance of this name? It comes from the verb "to be" in the Hebrew. Therefore, it is tied to the idea of life itself. "To be" is "to live." "To be" at its very essence is to have life. Thus the name implies that God is absolutely self-existent. He is the One who in Himself possesses life and permanent existence. He alone!

Sometimes our children ask us, "Well, Daddy (or Mommy), who created God?" And we reply with profound wisdom and confidence, "In the beginning was God." Unsatisfied they repeat, "But who created God?" When such a question is asked, it is obvious that we are thinking in a scientific fashion in terms of cause and effect. We have been taught that everything that exists had to have a prior cause. That is the point of the name Yahweh. God is the uncaused cause. He is the first cause and before Him there was no other and after Him there will be no other. Life is found in Him. He is the first cause that you may have been searching for all of your life.

During Israel's exile in Babylon, Daniel rebuked Belshazzar, the pagan king. He declared: "But you have exalted yourself against the Lord of heaven; . . . and you have praised the gods of silver and gold, of bronze, iron, wood and stone, which do not see, hear or understand. But the God in whose hand are your life-breath and your ways, you have not glorified" (5:23). The king's mistake was a fundamental one. He worshiped the gods of his own making, but ignored the God who had made him.

Yahweh alone is God; before Him, nothing existed, and without Him there is no life. Nothing exists except that it has its life in Him, and we will never understand our purpose as a human race or as human beings until we know Him.

The Revelation of the Name Yahweh

Exodus 3 is the most critical passage for our understanding of the name Yahweh. The children of Israel were slaves in Egypt and had been crying out to God for deliverance. Then God confronted Moses by speaking to him from a burning bush. This account of the calling of Moses is one of the most striking and convincing events in the Bible.

When the Lord saw that Moses had turned aside to look at the bush, He called to him from the midst of the bush, telling Moses that he was standing on holy ground. It is not insignificant that God first identified Himself in terms of His historic relationship to Israel's forefathers. "He said also, 'I am the God of your father, the God of Abraham, the God of Isaac, and the God of Jacob'" (Exod. 3:6). In humility and fear, Moses hid his face, for he was afraid to look upon God. No doubt Moses knew the great stories of God's supernatural activity among His chosen people.

Now this same God was saying to Moses that the God who had acted redemptively and powerfully in the lives of the patriarchs was speaking to him in the present tense. By this historic reference, He was reminding Moses that He had delivered His people in the past, He had sustained and cared for them through the years. Next He made the incredible announcement that He was about to act in the present to deliver Israel from Egyptian captivity. He promised Moses that He had come down to deliver Israel from the hand of the Egyptians and to bring them to a spacious and fruitful land (3:8).

The revelation takes an unexpected turn when God declares His intention to use Moses as His instrument for deliverance. "Therefore, come now, and I will send you to Pharaoh, so that you may bring My people, the sons of Israel, out of Egypt" (3:10). Moses, not thrilled with this news, immediately objected that he was incapable and unworthy to participate in such a venture. "But Moses said to God, 'Who am I, that I should go to

Pharaoh, and that I should bring the sons of Israel out of Egypt?'" (3:11).

Moses' question, "Who am I?" is both irrelevant and irreverent, because God had already promised that He Himself would deliver Israel. Moses was merely chosen to be an instrument in the hands of God. The question is irreverent because it calls into question God's judgment in His choice of such a lowly and incompetent servant. Moses gave God excuses about his inability to speak or to stand before the Pharaoh. Who could imagine the created one arguing against the Creator? Yet don't we find ourselves in a similar situation today? We're called upon to teach a class, witness to a friend, or some other task of service, and we reply, "Who am I?" We make excuses about our inability and we question God's right or wisdom in calling us to serve Him. We, like Moses, suffer from the mistaken idea that we can do God's work in our own strength. When God calls us to a task, we can rest assured that He has created us for this very purpose and will empower us to accomplish it.

HE IS ACTIVE IN THE PRESENT

I believe that Moses asked such an irrelevant and irreverent question because he suffered from a problem that affects men and women today. Until God approached Moses at the burning bush, He was only a God of history to Moses, not a God of the present. Perhaps Moses had absolute confidence that God had worked miraculously in the lives of Abraham, Isaac, and Jacob. He probably never would have considered calling these historical accounts into question. Yet, at the moment of truth, he struggled to believe that the God of history could work through his life to deliver Israel.

Tragically, many of us are at the same point in our Christian pilgrimages. We have no problem affirming the historical accuracy of the Bible. We don't question that God opened the Red Sea. We may not be sure how He accomplished this feat or how wide the opening was, but we're sure it was big enough to get the children of Israel through on dry land. We believe that God fed the five thousand with five loaves and two fishes. We believe that all the miracles are historically true!

What if you were asked: "Do you believe that God can work in your life today? Do you believe He can use you to change your nation? Do you believe that God can work in your church today to transform your city and the world? Do you believe that God can change your marriage and restore broken relationships? Do you believe that God can forgive your sin? Do you believe that God can work in your life, enabling you to teach that Sunday school class? Do you believe that God can work in your life to reach that unsaved friend that you've been thinking is beyond His reach?" Is your God merely a God of history, and not necessarily a God of the present?

Then Moses asked a second question, and it's a good one. In truth, it is the only question that has any relevance in his life or in ours. "Then Moses said to God, 'Behold, I am going to the sons of Israel, and I shall say to them, "The God of your fathers has sent me to you." Now they may say to me, "What is His name?" What shall I say to them?'" (3:13). That is a great question. It is both relevant and reverent. It is the question that should be the focus of our attention as we grow in our relationship to God.

In verse 14, God answers him: "And God said to Moses, 'I AM WHO I AM'; and He said, 'Thus you shall say to the sons of Israel, "I AM has sent me to you."' And God, furthermore, said to Moses, 'Thus you shall say to the sons of Israel, "The LORD, the God of your fathers, the God of Abraham, the God of Isaac, and the God of Jacob, has sent me to you." This is My name forever, and this is my memorial name to all the generations.'"

Various scholars have suggested different translations of the name of God used in this passage. The name is from the imperfect stem of the Hebrew verb "to be." The imperfect tense denotes an action that started in the past, continues in the present, but is not yet complete. Many Bible scholars follow the simple translation that we have in our text, "I am who I am." One of our Old Testament scholars at Southwestern translates it this way: "I AM who I have always been." I like this translation because it affirms that the God who spoke from the burning bush is the same God who worked through the lives of Abraham, Isaac, and Jacob. It also implies His ability and desire to work through Moses in the present and the future. However we translate this name, we can be assured that it affirms God's self-existence and His eternality.

THE GOD OF REVELATION

We first encountered the name Yahweh in Genesis 2:4, but with no explanation of its meaning. Here in Exodus, Moses, the author of the first five books of the Bible, shows us the significance of God's name by connecting it to the covenant and a promise to the people. He affirms that the God of creation is the God of the patriarchs who has now manifested Himself as a personal, living God who will fulfill to the people of Israel the promise that He made to their fathers. The name Jehovah declares that God is personal, self-existent, and unchanging in

His desire to reveal Himself in the personal redemption of those He has created (cf. Exod. 6:3–6).

As we study the Old Testament, we will find that the name Yahweh is used consistently in passages involving revelation. You don't find references that begin, "Thus saith Elohim." It is always "Thus saith Yahweh, or Jehovah." This name affirms that God not only exists but that He communicates with us. He desires to reveal Himself in such a way that we can come to know Him.

Through revelation He inspired the prophets to speak the very words of God. Beyond this, we know that God ultimately revealed Himself by taking on human flesh in the person of Jesus of Nazareth. When you read the Gospel of John, you will discover numerous "I am" statements from the mouth of Jesus. You will recall that He declared Himself to be the bread of life; the living water; the way, the truth, and the life. The Jewish listeners of Jesus' day could not have helped but connect these "I am" declarations with the great "I AM" affirmation of God in the Old Testament. Jesus was declaring to His audience that He was God in the flesh. It is no wonder that many Jews accused Him of blasphemy. We should not overlook the precious truth that Jesus is fully God. He is the I AM. Thus it is true that if we are to know Jehovah in a personal way, we can do so only through His Son.

THE GOD OF RIGHTEOUSNESS AND HOLINESS

The name Jehovah or Yahweh also underlines God's moral and spiritual attributes. We can now see that Jehovah has covenanted with men based on the credibility of His own moral and spiritual attributes. The first reference to the name Jehovah, in

Genesis 2:4, is found in conjunction with the name Elohim, the Maker of the heavens and the earth.

Moses, the inspired author of Genesis and Exodus, wanted us to understand that there is only one God. We must not be confused as we go through this study. We do not have a pantheon of gods. We worship one God, the Creator of the heavens and the earth, who is a holy God, who reveals Himself in such a manner that we can know Him in a personal relationship. The name Yahweh emphasizes the moral nature of the covenant God of Israel.

It is interesting that when Satan tempted Eve to sin (Gen. 3:1–5), he refers to God as Elohim. When Eve responds to Satan, she also uses the name Elohim. In Genesis 3:8–9, after Adam and Eve had sinned, they hear the word and the voice of *Yahweh*. "And they heard the sound of the LORD God walking in the garden in the cool of the day, and the man and his wife hid themselves from the presence of the LORD God [Yahweh Elohim] among the trees of the garden."

The name Yahweh underscores that God is holy and righteous. The psalmist declares:

> For the LORD [Yahweh] is righteous;
> He loves righteousness;
> The upright will behold His face. (Ps. 11:7)

Daniel 9:14 is also instructive: "'For the LORD our God [Yahweh our Elohim] is righteous with respect to all His deeds which He has done, but we have not obeyed His voice.'" In the very next verse, Daniel refers to the great deliverance of the Exodus and contrasts it with the sin of God's people. "'And now, O Lord our God, who has brought Thy people out of the land of Egypt with a mighty hand and hast made a name for Thyself, as it is this day—we have sinned, we have been wicked.'" Daniel 9:14 says that "'[Jehovah, our Elohim] is righteous with respect to all His deeds.'" In Leviticus 19:2, the first requirement of those who would follow Him is that "you shall be holy for [Yahweh, your Elohim] (is) holy."

We must understand that when we sin, it is against the righteousness of God. It is not ultimately that we violate man's standards. There is only one moral standard in the universe that counts and that is the standard of the Creator, Yahweh or Elohim. He Himself is righteousness and therefore it is against the righteousness of a holy God that man's sin must be understood.

The name Yahweh is used when God drives Adam and Eve from the garden. The incredibly good news of Scripture is that Yahweh, who is holy, is also characterized by His love in relationship with His people. In Jeremiah 31:3 we read:

> The LORD [Yahweh] appeared to him from afar, saying,
> "I have loved you with an everlasting love;
> Therefore I have drawn you with lovingkindness."

As a holy God, Yahweh must condemn sin, because it destroys His very image in man, who was created for relationship with a holy God. Yet, in His love, He has provided a way for man's redemption.

Let us return to our primary passage in Exodus, chapter 3. You will remember that we were told that Yahweh was the memorial name by which Israel was to know God. The content of that story focused on God's redemption of His people. Look again at verses 8 and 10. In verse 8, God declares that He has come down to deliver or redeem Israel. In verse 10, He commissions Moses to go to Pharaoh to bring forth God's people from captivity. For all who find themselves captive to sin today and think that there would be no way they could approach a holy God, this story brings good news. Yahweh has the power to redeem you and bring you out of your captivity.

THE PROMISE OF REDEMPTION

One of the great passages of redemption in the Old Testament is Exodus 34, where we find recorded the story of Moses receiving the Ten Commandments, the moral code of righteousness by which Israel was called to live. If you are a student of Old Testament history, you will recall that this was the second time God had inscribed these commandments on stone tablets. Moses had shattered the original tablets when he descended from the mountain and looked upon the sin of Israel as they worshiped the golden calf (Exod. 32:15–20).

In Exodus 34, we are told that the Lord descended in the cloud and stood with Moses as he called upon His name. "Then the LORD passed by in front of him and proclaimed, 'The LORD, the LORD God, compassionate and gracious, slow to anger, and abounding in lovingkindness and truth; who keeps lovingkindness for thousands, who forgives iniquity, transgression and sin; yet He will by no means leave the guilty unpunished.'" (vv. 6–7a). Notice the integral connection between the attributes of God, His judgment of sin, and His promise of forgiveness. Because God is a holy God, he must condemn sin. There are those who want to argue that if God were truly loving, He would never condemn sinners. Such an argument misses the point completely. Because God is both holy and loving, He must condemn sin, because its effect is to destroy His image in us. That's what Paul means when He declares that the wages of sin is death. Sin causes spiritual death and separation from our holy God. For God to be holy, He must also be just, and His justice leads to the condemnation of sin. At the same time, His lovingkindness, His compassionate nature, offers us forgiveness from sin.

God's Sacrifice for Sin

The Book of Leviticus in the Old Testament is powerful and precious because it deals with a system of sacrifice by which man could be made clean before God. As we read about the grain offerings, the sin offerings, the turtledoves and heifers, we may sometimes find it slow and confusing reading, but we should not fail to see the truth of God's great love offering man a way of cleansing from sin.

You may find it fascinating that in the first seven chapters of Leviticus, which sets forth this system of sacrifice, the name Elohim is used only one time, while the name Yahweh is used eighty-six times. In Leviticus 16, which is about the great Day of Atonement, there are twelve references to the name of God, and each time it is Yahweh. In other words, it is in Yahweh that we will find our redemption and our atonement.

We have already mentioned the great "I AM" sayings in John's Gospel, which declare that Jesus is the very incarnation of Yahweh. Jesus clearly articulated the truth that He and the Father were one (John 10:30) and that He alone provided eternal access to the Father (John 14:6). The Book of Hebrews further tells us that Jesus Himself became the fulfillment of the sacrificial system outlined in the Old Testament. Take time to read all of Hebrews 10, this wonderful account of God's fulfilled promise:

> After saying above, "SACRIFICES AND OFFER-
> INGS AND WHOLE BURNT OFFERINGS AND SACRI-
> FICES FOR SIN THOU HAS NOT DESIRED, NOR HAST
> THOU TAKEN PLEASURE IN THEM" (which are
> offered according to the Law), then He said,
> "Behold I have come to do thy will." He takes away
> the first in order to establish the second. By this
> will we have been sanctified through the offering
> of the body of Jesus Christ once for all. And every
> priest stands daily ministering and offering time
> after time the same sacrifices, which can never take
> away sins; but He, having offered one sacrifice for
> sins for all time, SAT DOWN AT THE RIGHT HAND OF
> GOD. (vv. 8–12)

Jesus' sacrifice of Himself on the cross was the single sacri-fice that accomplished what the daily sacrifices could only point to in the future. That makes the wonderful assurance of Hebrews 10:18 possible for the believer today. "Now where there is for-giveness of these things, there is no longer any offering for sin." For that very reason we have confidence to enter into God's presence by the blood of Jesus (10:19). Thus we can draw near with a sincere heart and full assurance of faith (10:22). The blood of Jesus refers to His self-giving on the cross to forgive us of our sins (Heb. 13:11–12).

THE NEED FOR YAHWEH TODAY

The tragedy in our day is that many people are still attempting to please God by their own merit. They are aware of their own sinful condition, but they hope they can be good enough or attend church frequently enough to atone for their sin. Others have looked to New Age philosophies for comfort, thinking that they might be reincarnated and have another chance at life. The Bible alone promises the only sure solution to our sin problem. We have been offered forgiveness by God Himself. If we are to approach a holy God, we must do so on His terms. Since none are righteous and all are guilty of sin, a sinless sacrifice was required. God in His great love sent His own Son. "For God so loved the world, that He gave his only begotten Son, that whoever believes in Him should not perish, but have eternal life" (John 3:16).

The only thing that will make a difference when you stand before God is how you responded to His offer of forgiveness through His Son. It will not matter where you attended church, or what denomination you identified with, or how many good things you did. God's forgiveness is a free gift made possible in His Son. When you have experienced forgiveness and live in a personal relationship with the Creator of the world, you will discover that He is a God of the present tense, continually working in your life. Therefore you will find that you hunger to know Him more through the study of His Word and through fellowship with others who are in relationship with Him. You will want to tell others of the wonderful discovery you have made so that they may know their Creator in a personal way.

When we have received Christ, we must come to understand the same lesson that Moses had to learn—that God is "I AM" in the present tense of our lives. Do you know God as active in your life to overcome doubt or depression? Do you know Him as the *present tense* answer to the healing of broken relationships? Do you know Him as the God who can deal with your anger and resentment, as the God who can change your life? He is the "I AM" who is active to transform and empower daily living. Whatever your present tense need, Jesus is the "I AM" of God.

Some truths may seem so deep that our human mind struggles with them, but we must understand that God revealed Himself personally and fully in Jesus Christ. It was Christ who was God from the very beginning, who became flesh, and who took upon Himself our sin that we might take upon ourselves the righteousness of God. Yahweh is the God of the present tense; the God of redemption, the God who has revealed Himself fully in Christ Jesus. He alone is the definition of God, who has life, and has come to live in us today.

6

JEHOVAH JIREH

THE LORD
PROVIDES

And Abraham called the name of that place
The LORD Will Provide, as it is said to this day,
"In the mount of the LORD it will be provided."

GENESIS 22:14

As a former athlete, I love sporting events. Of course, I want to see my team win, but I must confess that I still like the event to have a sense of drama. I like to see the game go to the bottom of the ninth, with two outs and the bases loaded and my team three runs down. Then, of course, I like to see the clean-up hitter deliver a grand slam.

"Bottom of the ninth" experiences happen in everyday life, also. We come to that point where we must deliver when the game is on the line. In this chapter, our study deals with just such an event in the life of Abraham. In this "bottom of the ninth" experience, God reveals Himself as *Jehovah Jireh,* the God who provides.

A FINAL FAITH HURDLE

This event is told with a sense of drama unparalleled in all of Scripture. All the other tests of Abraham's faith pale in comparison to this final test. They look like little more than a prelude to the staggering command of God. The first phrase, "Now it came about after these things," tells you that this is the culmination of Abraham's faith experience. The author wants us to call to mind Abraham's entire journey of faith.

When God had called Abram to leave his native land and occupy a new land that He would show him, He also promised to bless Abram and to make him a blessing. Part of the blessing was that He promised He would make of Abram a mighty nation.

Time passed and God continued to bless Abram and Sarai, but still they had no children of their own. When God repeated His promise to Abram, reminding him that his reward would be great (Gen. 15:1), Abram suggested that he could adopt his

servant Eliezer as his heir. Apparently Abram felt God needed
help in fulfilling His promise. In an act of desperation and disobedience the child Ishmael was born to Abram and Sarai's
handmaiden, Hagar (Gen. 16:1–4). When Abram was ninety-
nine years old, God reaffirmed His covenant. God's promise to
make Abram the father of many nations may have seemed
impossible and perhaps a reproach since the name Abram
meant "exalted father," and he did not have a single child. Here
God appeared to him as El Shaddai, the God who is almighty
to nourish, renewing his covenant and changing Abram's name
to Abraham, the father of a multitude. Then the child of promise, Isaac, the beloved child of his own flesh, was born. After this
journey of faith, God came to Abraham with a final test to see
if Abraham had learned to trust Him to provide his every need.

When God calls to Abraham, he answers without delay. The
command is told in an unadorned fashion, which belies the
enormity of the request. "'Take now your son, your only son,
whom you love, Isaac, and go to the land of Moriah; and offer
him there as a burnt offering on one of the mountains of which
I will tell you'" (Gen. 22:2). Did you notice the repetition of the
word *son* connected with the name Isaac? It is not merely *a* son
that God requires of Abraham, it is *his only son,* it is Isaac, the son
whom he loved. It is the son who was the crucial foundation stone
for the fulfillment of the promise that Abraham would become
the father of many nations. This was not only a staggering faith
commitment; it was an enormous personal challenge.

A few years ago, we moved from Atlanta to Fort Worth,
where I was to assume the presidency of Southwestern
Seminary. Our youngest daughter, Katie, and I had to go to Fort
Worth before the rest of the family could join us. At the same
time, our middle daughter, Rachael, was entering Samford

University in Birmingham, Alabama, as a freshman. One of the reasons we had selected that particular school was because of its proximity to Atlanta. Rachael has always loved being close to home and Samford seemed like a perfect college choice until God called the rest of the family to move to Texas.

Rachael moved to Birmingham one weekend (without Dad's assistance) and our home in Atlanta sold the next weekend. The transition was difficult for the entire family, but especially for Rachael. To say that she was homesick was an understatement. A few months after the term began, I found an opportunity to visit my daughter in Birmingham. After a short, two-day visit, I had to return to Texas to resume work. When I put out my arms to hug Rachael good-bye, she clung to me and sobbed like her heart was breaking. I could feel the convulsions of her body as she thought about our separation and the months before the next holiday break.

A few years later, our family was standing in an airport lobby in Bulgaria. The entire family had journeyed to Bulgaria to visit Kristina, our eldest daughter, who was serving there as a Journeyman missionary, and now we were returning to the United States. We knew that it would be more than a year before we would see our daughter again. We also knew that the living conditions would be challenging for a single young lady. Once again, as I had back in Birmingham, I found myself sobbing along with a child of my own flesh, whom I was giving up for a short time. As I left her, I thought of Abraham's experience with Isaac and the incredible personal struggle they both must have experienced.

To make matters worse, Abraham wasn't just saying good-bye to a child that he expected to see again in a few months or a year, he was expecting to sacrifice his only son on an altar

before the Lord. Yet, the text simply states: "So Abraham rose early in the morning and saddled his donkey, and took two of his young men with him and Isaac his son; and he split wood for the burnt offering, and arose and went to the place of which God had told him" (Gen. 22:3). Abraham's response was immediate obedience. Not one word of objection is recorded in the entire text. No doubt he was struggling with a deep inner turmoil, but he had learned to walk with God and to trust Him to provide.

Abraham's Maturing Faith

Abraham's growing faith, which had been fortified when God Almighty brought forth life from Sarah's dead and barren womb, was now sufficient for the journey to Mt. Moriah. After he and Isaac had traveled three days and the mountain was in sight, Abraham instructed the young men with him and Isaac to stay behind with the donkey. Listen to his promise, uttered by faith: "I and the lad will go yonder; and we will worship and return to you" (Gen. 22:5b). He tells the young men that after he and his son worship on Mt. Moriah, they both will return.

If we look ahead to the New Testament, the author of Hebrews gives us an insight into Abraham's thoughts when he took his son to Mt. Moriah to offer him as a sacrifice. "By faith Abraham, when he was tested, offered up Isaac; and he who had received the promises was offering up his only begotten son; it was he to whom it was said, 'IN ISAAC YOUR DESCENDANTS SHALL BE CALLED.' He considered that God is able to raise men even from the dead; from which he also received him back as a type" (Heb. 11:17–19).

The concept of resurrection of the dead had not been mentioned previously in the first twenty-one chapters of Genesis.

Today, we can look upon resurrection with a sense of assurance, because we believe that Jesus was raised from the dead. But Abraham dared to believe that the God he served, who had brought life to a barren womb, could raise Isaac from the dead even though such a miracle had never before occurred. Nevertheless, Abraham had grown to understand that God was trustworthy and faithful concerning all His promises. Therefore, he believed that God sought only good for him and for Isaac. He had come to the point that he was willing to trust God with the most valued possession of his life, his only son Isaac.

God Will Provide

Father and son continued on their fateful journey to Mt. Moriah. Finally, the son interrupts what may have been an awkward silence. Isaac asks his father a logical question if they are going to Mt. Moriah to worship and then return. "Behold, the fire and the wood, but where is the lamb for the burnt offering?" (Gen. 22:7b). Abraham's simple response is a verbal expression of his growing faith. "And Abraham said, 'God will provide for Himself the lamb for the burnt offering, my son.' So the two of them walked on together" (22:8).

The text gives us no clue as to the time that might have passed between verse 8 and verse 9; but in verse 9, the journey is at its conclusion. The pair had arrived at the place that God had designated for the sacrifice. Father and son prepared the altar together and arranged the wood for the sacrifice. I have often wondered if any dialogue passed between Abraham and Isaac. The text is silent. We are simply told that Abraham bound his son and laid him on the altar, then took a knife in his hand to slay him. Even as we read the story, we are nearly breathless. We are convinced that Abraham is committed to obeying the

command of God, even though he may not fully comprehend its import. He has grown in his faith to the point where he knows that God will provide for his every need.

It is precisely at this moment, as Abraham wields the knife, that the angel of the Lord called to him from heaven. I am confident that the divine interrupter calling out his name must have been the sweetest words to strike mortal ears. The angel's message: "Do not stretch out your hand against the lad, and do nothing to him; for now I know that you fear God, since you have not withheld your son, your only son, from Me" (22:12).

We have found throughout this study that our circumstances never test the credibility or the faithfulness of God, they serve only to test our understanding of the character and purpose of God in our life. Thus, as Abraham raised the knife, it was evident that he revered God and trusted Him with his most precious possession—his only son.

Now Abraham raised his eyes, looking away from the trusting eyes of his son, and saw behind him in the thicket a ram caught by its horns. Abraham realized that this was the Lord's provision for a sacrifice in the place of his son. "And Abraham called the name of that place 'The LORD will Provide,' as it is said to this day, 'In the mount of the LORD, it will be provide'" (22:14). This is the name Jehovah Jireh.

The Hebrew word *jireh* can be translated "to see." You wonder what the connection is between "seeing" and "providing." Actually we can make the connection even in the English noun *provision*. It is a compound of two Latin words which taken together mean "to see beforehand." Thus "pro-vision" would mean "to see beforehand." In God's case, He had anticipated, or seen beforehand, Abraham's need for a sacrifice and thus had personally provided one.

Before the foundation of the world, God had prior vision of man's later sin and rebellion. Seeing man's need, He made provision for our redemption by providing a lamb of sacrifice, His only Son. The parallels are striking indeed between this passage of provision for Abraham and a later provision when another Son was stretched out on an altar made of a Roman cross. Both events show us that God alone can provide for man's needs. We are not self-sufficient. We are God-dependent, and the sooner we discover that wonderful truth, the sooner we will find the strength for daily living.

Abraham's joyous response in the naming of the place Jehovah Jireh must be held in stark contrast to the deep faith questions that must have perplexed his soul as he journeyed to that place. Has God really spoken to me? Can He be trusted with my everyday affairs? Can I give Him my son, the son of the covenant? Indeed the answer is yes, yes, yes. He is Jehovah Jireh, the God who provides. Now Abraham could receive his son back, not just as a beloved son, but as a gracious gift from God the Provider, entrusted to Abraham in stewardship.

God's Blessings Unleashed

This story is so powerful and dramatic that we are tempted to stop reading at this point. But the revelation is not complete. The angel of the LORD called to Abraham a second time and said: "By Myself I have sworn, declares the LORD, because you have done this thing, and have not withheld your son, your only son, indeed I will greatly bless you, and I will greatly multiply your seed as the stars of the heavens, and as the sand which is on the seashore; and your seed shall possess the gate of their enemies. And in your seed all the nations of the earth shall be blessed, because you have obeyed My voice" (Gen. 22:16–18).

Abraham's obedience unleashed God's blessing in his life. Obedience is the key to faith. Faith comes by hearing and hearing by the Word of God. But true hearing in the life of the believer is accompanied by a response of obedience. James speaks to this issue with great clarity. He insists that we must be doers and not just hearers of the word. "For if anyone is a hearer of the word and not a doer, he is like a man who looks at his natural face in a mirror; for once he has looked at himself and gone away, he has immediately forgotten what kind of person he was. But one who looks intently at the perfect law, the law of liberty, and abides by it, not having become a forgetful hearer but an effectual doer, this man shall be blessed in what he does" (James 1:23–25). If you want to unleash God's blessing in your life, if you want to discover that God is Provider, then you must obey. Abraham's obedience was immediate and unqualified.

Let me give you two little statements about obedience that may help you. Delayed obedience is immediate disobedience. Partial obedience is complete disobedience. Are there issues where you have only partially obeyed what God has commanded? Are there matters where you have tried to make a deal with God that at some point in the future you will obey Him? "I'll start tithing when I get a better job or pay off my debt." Such delayed obedience is nothing more than disobedience and it robs us of the joy of discovering that God is Jehovah Jireh.

P. S. Don't miss the last verse of this section. "So Abraham returned to his young men, and they arose and went together to Beersheba; and Abraham lived at Beersheba" (Gen. 22:19). Abraham had told the young men that after he and Isaac had worshiped, they would return. God is sufficient to provide our every need and fulfill His every promise if we will only trust and obey.

GOD CAN BE TRUSTED WITH YOUR "ISAAC"

Have you come to the place in your faith pilgrimage where you know that you can trust God with your "Isaac"? Your Isaac may be your career, your family, a relationship, your retirement, your college plans, or the provision for tomorrow. What has become the focus of your life? Do you believe that God can provide for your needs? Are you willing to place your Isaac upon the altar?

There is an interesting verse in John 3. You may know that this passage is about an encounter between Jesus and Nicodemus, a Pharisee and ruler of the Jews. We remember this passage mostly for Jesus' statement that Nicodemus must be born again. When Nicodemus tells Jesus that he doesn't understand how he can be born again, Jesus responds in verse 12: "If I told you earthly things and you do not believe, how shall you believe if I tell you heavenly things?" Chances are, you have already trusted Christ for your salvation. In other words, you are trusting Him for issues relating to where you will spend eternity. But if you can trust God for eternal issues, then why do you struggle with earthly things when God has given such clear instructions?

Jesus confronted His disciples on the issue of trust. He told them that His followers did not need to be anxious about food, rent, or clothing. He then instructed them to look at the lilies of the field, which do not express any anxiety about their clothing and yet are beautifully arrayed. Jesus' advice to the disciples: "But seek first His kingdom and His righteousness; and all these things shall be added to you" (Matt. 6:33). If you can trust God to provide for your eternity, why is it such a challenge to trust Him with your tomorrow?

Surveys indicate that less than 20 percent of those who call themselves evangelical Christians have learned to trust God in their financial stewardship. We are taught that we are to live anxiety-free lives, yet many Christians are fraught with worry about the future, their children, their marriages, or their security. Paul simply counsels: "Be anxious for nothing, but in everything by prayer and supplication with thanksgiving let your requests be made known to God. And the peace of God, which surpasses all comprehension, shall guard your hearts and your minds in Christ Jesus" (Phil. 4:6–7).

Our ability to claim and live by God's promise will come only when we have experienced Him as Jehovah Jireh. We must first understand the character of God, then we must willingly place our Isaac upon the altar of sacrifice, and allow God to be our Provider.

When I was in college, I was privileged to attend a Fellowship of Christian Athletes camp and hear the testimony of Bobby Richardson, one of the finest second basemen ever to play the game of baseball. Bobby had the good fortune to grow up in a fine Christian home. Early in life, he had set as a goal to play professional baseball and thereby to obtain his fame and fortune. One day, early in Bobby's career, the starting second baseman was removed from a game because of an injury. Bobby stepped in and experienced immediate success. Day after day, he performed well offensively and defensively. By the time the regular second baseman was ready to return to the lineup, Bobby had beaten him out for the position.

The next year, he was signed to an excellent, long-term contract. He continued to play well and soon was an all-star. He had achieved all that he had dreamed about. He now had his fame and fortune, but life seemed empty. One night, in a hotel room, he crawled down beside the bed on his knees and took his baseball glove from his duffel bag. In deep agony of soul, he laid the glove on the bed and poured out his heart before God. He was willing to give up baseball if that was what was required to find fulfillment in his life. Bobby's "Isaac" was the baseball career he had been seeking all his life. He had discovered that playing baseball had possessed him. Once he placed it before the Lord in total surrender, he found that he could trust God to provide for his every need. It was only after this "Mt. Moriah" experience that Bobby was able to fully enjoy the opportunity to use his baseball ability for the glory of the Lord.

Do you remember what happened in Abraham's life after the encounter with God on Mt. Moriah? All of God's promises were released in his life. He knew the blessings of Jehovah Jireh. Too many of us are missing the joy of seeing God's blessings fully released in our lives because we are tenaciously clinging to that which seems most precious. We argue with God that we can't possibly put our career or our family on the altar, because it is the only thing we have of value. The problem is that we have taken *possession* of what God gave to us *in stewardship,* and we have failed to understand the fullness that God desires to bring to our life.

This week, take several practical steps and see what God shows you about Himself.

1. Practice immediate obedience.
2. Learn to trust Him to be fully consistent with His nature.
3. Believe that He is Jehovah Jireh, the God who provides.
4. Place that which is most cherished in your life on the altar. Surrender it completely to Him.
5. Be prepared to praise Him whether He restores your Isaac or removes it. Remember He is God, fully loving and altogether trustworthy.
6. Practice these principles daily.

7

JEHOVAH ROPHE

THE LORD HEALS

"I will put none of the diseases on you which I have brought on the Egyptians. For I am the LORD who heals you."

EXODUS 15:26B, NKJV

One of the most popular movies of early 1999 was *The Prince of Egypt*. It was an animated story based on the life of Moses. The Exodus is one of the most significant events in Old Testament history. One of the most powerful scenes in the movie is the depiction of the parting of the Red Sea. Moses had just led the children of Israel out of Egyptian bondage. Once the people had left the land, Pharaoh changed his mind and pursued the fleeing Israelites. The children of Israel were blocked in front by the Red Sea and behind by the oncoming Egyptian army. Moses, the leader of Israel, held the rod of God out over the sea and the waters were piled up on both sides. The people of Israel marched through on dry land and then the waters returned, drowning the Egyptian army.

God had exhibited His power to lead a nation from captivity into freedom. As they reached the other shore they began to sing praises to the Lord for His deliverance. You can find this song in Exodus 15. Let me give you a sample:

> "I will sing to the LORD, for He is highly exalted;
> The horse and its rider He has hurled into the sea.
> The LORD is my strength and song,
> And He has become my salvation;
> This is my God, and I will praise Him;
> My father's God, and I will extol Him.
> The LORD is a warrior;
> The LORD is His name." (vv. 2–3)

Several of the names that we have already studied are used in various portions of this song. The name Yahweh occurs with great regularity. Moses then refers to Him as his father's Elohim. It is a moving and powerful song of victory. It is precisely what we would expect as the people stood victoriously on the safe side of the Red Sea. But as we follow the story we will discover that the theme of victory is soon lost and the people begin to complain as they travel through the wilderness. It is at a critical moment in the journey that God reveals another facet of His character in the unveiling of the name *Jehovah Rophe.*

THE JOURNEY TO MARAH

Several days into the journey, the people of Israel began to grumble and complain. They were frustrated by the lack of food and water. They began to argue that they would be better off in the brick pits of Egypt. Does it surprise you that great spiritual victory is often followed by defeat, discouragement, dissension, and depression? Satan often intensifies his spiritual attack immediately after we experience spiritual victory. He always tries to snatch away our victory and attempts to dull our joy.

The Bitter Waters of Marah

As the last notes of the song of victory faded away, Moses led Israel into the wilderness of Shur. They went three days in the wilderness and found no water. The way was difficult, conditions were hot and dry. Water was scarce, and on the third day, suffering from physical thirst, they began to forget the mercy and provision of God, who had delivered them at the Red Sea. Their physical condition began to impact their spiritual joy. Nothing is more paralyzing than thirst.

Then they saw Marah in the distance and at first it appeared to offer a solution to their problem. Perhaps they saw the palm trees marking an oasis with its life-giving wells. Their hope was dashed to pieces, though, when they discovered that the wells of

Marah contained bitter water. The water could not satisfy their thirst or supply their need for life-giving water.

The people grumbled at Moses, asking what they would drink. Moses cried to the Lord in his desperation: "Then he cried out to the LORD, and the LORD showed him a tree; and he threw it into the waters, and the waters became sweet. There He made for them a statute and regulation, and there He tested them. And He said, 'If you will give earnest heed to the voice of the LORD your God, and do what is right in His sight, and give ear to His commandments, and keep all His statutes, I will put none of the diseases on you which I have put on the Egyptians; for I, the LORD, am your healer'" (Exod. 15:25–26). It was at this point that they discovered that Yahweh is also Jehovah Rophe, the God who heals. Leaving Marah, they made their way to Elim, where they found twelve springs of fresh water and seventy date palms. God took them from Marah to Elim and gave them an abundant supply of water. The crisis wass now passed and they had discovered that the Lord can turn the bitter water to sweet.

THE MEANING OF JEHOVAH ROPHE

The word *rophe* occurs about sixty times in the Old Testament and it always means "to restore," "to heal," or "to cure." It is frequently used in relation to physical healing. It can also be used to relate to moral and spiritual healing. Jehovah reveals Himself to be the only source of wholeness. He alone has the power to change the bitter experiences of life into sweet.

It appears once again that God has demonstrated His ability to provide for Israel's needs. Is that what happened? Is it up to God to demonstrate anything? Who was being tested at Marah?

Often we think that our difficult circumstances put God to the test. The truth is that our circumstances test us. God is the same yesterday, today, and forever. God is never put to the test. He has proved Himself from the beginning. He is Creator and Lord. He is the sovereign God of the universe. His nature and character are unchanging. God is not tested by circumstances. Yet God, in conformity with His own character, turns the bitter circumstances of our life into sweet.

Notice the conclusion of verse 25: "There He made for them a statute and regulation, and there He tested them." Their test is the same one we face today. They had to listen to the voice of the Lord, do what was right, and obey His commandments. That is the pattern for victory when we face bitter circumstances which might otherwise bring discouragement and disillusionment. Listen to God and obey His commands.

WHAT DO YOU DO WHEN YOU GET TO MARAH?

When you experience the difficult circumstances of life, when you come to a place where disillusionment and bitterness fill the wells of your life, remember that God can turn them sweet. Your bitter circumstances actually test you and teach you to trust God to meet every need of your life.

How should we respond when we find ourselves drinking from the wells of Marah? Let me make three specific suggestions. First, listen earnestly to the voice of God. What is God trying to say to you in your present circumstances? Sometimes we tend to hear God clearly when we are on the mountaintop of spiritual victory. When we get to Marah, we must tune our ears attentively to the voice of the Lord. Ask yourself what God is saying through your circumstances. What does God want to do in your life? What have you learned about God from these events?

Second, do what is right. In other words, behave righteously. Instead of responding by grumbling and complaining when you find yourself at Marah, do what is right. You can overcome your circumstances by focusing on the reliability of the nature of God. Because He never changes, you can know that He is loving and trustworthy and will meet your every need.

Third, obey God's commands. When you find yourself with bitter waters, look to see if there are areas of disobedience in your life. Our desire to obey Him emerges from the fact that we know His character. Thus our obedience is the response of joyous confidence.

OUR NEED OF HEALING

The astounding growth of hospitals, clinics, and counseling centers gives stark testimony to the prevalence of sickness and brokenness in our world. The newspaper headlines chronicle the rapid spread of diseases like AIDS and cancer. But our need for physical healing is small in comparison to our greater need for healing of emotions, relationships, and our spiritual condition. Violence has invaded our homes and our schools. It has become so commonplace that we are no longer shocked when we read of a thirteen-year-old turning a .22 rifle on his parents, or a sixteen-year-old, involved in satanic worship, taking his life in a school bathroom. All around us we see the ravages of sin and the need for healing.

Isaiah the prophet describes the problem of man's sickness as graphically as any writer in Scripture. He begins by chronicling the revolt of a people against their Creator and Master. They are depicted as being weighed down with iniquity, as sons who acted corruptly, who have turned away from their God. Then he asks:

> Where will you be stricken again,
> As you continue in your rebellion?
> The whole head is sick,
> And the whole heart is faint.
> From the sole of the foot even to the head
> There is nothing sound in it,
> Only bruises, welts, and raw wounds,
> Not pressed out or bandaged,
> Nor softened with oil. (Isa. 1:5–6)

Isaiah compares Israel to a physical body. There is no part of it which is healthy. It is covered with sores from head to foot with wounds and bruises and putrefying boils. Yet, in that same chapter, Isaiah holds out the possibility for healing. God can cleanse their scarlet sins and make them like snow. Then they will again eat the best of the land. The world needs to know that God is a God who heals. He can cure the deep wounds which sin has wrought. He is Jehovah Rophe.

GOD'S ACTIVITY IN HEALING

The Old Testament contains numerous stories of God's healing activity. In Numbers 12:13, we are told that Moses cried out on behalf of Miriam, who had been smitten with leprosy. "And Moses cried out to the LORD, saying, 'O God, heal her, I pray!'" The healing of Naaman's leprosy by Elisha is one of the most gripping stories in the Old Testament. The prophet required the proud king to dip himself in the Jordan seven times. When he humbled himself and followed Elisha's directions, the king's flesh was restored like the flesh of a child (2 Kings 5:8–14).

The prophet Jeremiah talks about sin and its consequences in terms of an incurable wound. The Lord through the prophet declares:

> "There is no one to plead your cause;
> No healing for your sore, no recovery for you."
> (Jer. 30:13)

He questions why they cry out over their injury when their pain is incurable and their sins are numerous. The Lord then declares:

> "For I will restore you to health
> And I will heal you of your wounds." (30:17)

When Jesus began His earthly ministry, he read from the prophet Isaiah:

> "THE SPIRIT OF THE LORD IS UPON ME,
> BECAUSE HE ANOINTED ME TO PREACH THE
>   GOSPEL TO THE POOR.
> HE HAS SENT ME TO PROCLAIM RELEASE TO THE
>   CAPTIVES,
> AND RECOVERY OF SIGHT TO THE BLIND,
> TO SET FREE THOSE WHO ARE OPPRESSED,
> TO PROCLAIM THE FAVORABLE YEAR OF THE
>   LORD." (Luke 4:18–19)

The healing miracles of Jesus abound in the Gospel narratives. We could point to the centurion's servant who was healed

by a word of command from a distance (Luke 7), the Gerasene who was cleansed of demonic possession (Luke 8), and the woman with the issue of blood who was healed while Jesus was on the way to heal Jarius's daughter (Luke 8), to name only a few of Jesus' healing miracles. Jesus was indeed the fulfillment of Jehovah Rophe. He turned the bitter waters to sweet in the lives of those to whom He ministered.

It is so easy for us to get so caught up in the stories of Jesus' healing ministry that we miss His clear priority for bringing healing in the spiritual realm. An event that clearly demonstrates this balance in the ministry of Jesus is found in Mark 1:29–38. Jesus heals Simon's mother-in-law of a fever. This created such interest that the whole city gathered at the door, bringing with them the sick and the demon-possessed. The next day, Jesus left the house early to spend time in prayer. The disciples sought Him out because the large crowd had returned seeking after Jesus. His response to the disciples points to His priority: "And He said to them, 'Let us go somewhere else to the towns nearby, so that I may preach there also; for that is what I came for'" (1:38). Jesus knew that His primary mission was to preach the good news of the deliverance from sin. He focused on the larger reality of spiritual healing. While physical healing was a compassionate ministry, it did not have the ultimate consequence of healing the alienation and spiritual death, that come as the result of sin.

A Balanced View for the Church Today

It appears to me that the church today would do well to follow the example of the Lord Jesus to keep evangelism as the focal point of its ministry strategy. Those churches that exalt the ministry of physical healing often become so caught up in the

mystique of such a ministry that they neglect the great task of offering ultimate healing from the wages of sin. As a consequence, they can become centered on the personality of the person who has the healing ministry rather than on Jehovah Rophe, who can alone bring healing. This pressure to produce healing results can often lead to exaggerated and unsubstantiated claims.

This doesn't mean that there is no place for intercessory prayer for healing in the ministry of our church today. Many churches invite folks to come to the altar if they need special prayer for healing. They do not advertise themselves as a healing church, nor do they make exaggerated claims. They simply but clearly ask God to intervene and bring healing. They are also clear to counsel people to seek good medical attention as they continue to pray and seek God's face.

I believe that James 5:13–16 gives clear instructions for a balanced ministry of prayer for healing. "Is anyone among you suffering? Let him pray. Is anyone cheerful? Let him sing praises. Is anyone among you sick? Let him call for the elders of the church, and let them pray over him, anointing him with oil in the name of the Lord; and the prayer offered in faith will restore the one who is sick, and the Lord will raise him up, and if he has committed sins, they will be forgiven him. Therefore, confess your sins to one another, and pray for one another, so that you may be healed. The effective prayer of a righteous man can accomplish much."

Notice the balance between prayer and praise, and healing and forgiveness. Further, you should notice that this is obviously a ministry of the local church. The sick are commanded to call for the church leaders. The context suggests both intimacy and accountability provided by the local church. For that reason, I

have never been an advocate of the massive healing crusades that are televised coast to coast. They lack the integrity and accountability provided by the local church context.

Let's follow now the sequence that is to take place in the local church. First, the healing ministry is initiated by the individual who is suffering. The suffering one is to pray in the same manner that the person celebrating should sing praises. We should always bring both our praise and our petitions before the Father.

Second, the sick person should call for the elders of the church. The elders clearly represent the spiritual leaders of the church. Depending on your church tradition, this should probably include the pastor, other staff members, and deacons or elders who are charged with the spiritual leadership of the church. The suggestion that the elders are summoned may well indicate that the actual praying and anointing with oil took place in the privacy of the home of the sick individual. The healing ministry of the early church was not conducted for the amusement or amazement of the onlookers, but for the compassionate care of the suffering.

Third, the elders are to pray over the individual and anoint him with oil. *Pray* is the main verb and *anoint* translates a participle. This suggests that prayer is the primary activity of the spiritual leaders of the church. The Greek word that is translated "anointing" may suggest that James had in mind a medicinal application of oil rather than a sacramental anointing. It is documented that oil was used medicinally in biblical times. Isaiah 1:6, cited earlier in this chapter, mentions the use of oil with bandages to soften a wound. Listen to this verse from the story of the Good Samaritan: "'But a certain Samaritan, who was on a journey, came upon him; and when he saw him, he

felt compassion, and came to him, and bandaged up his wounds, pouring oil and wine on them'" (Luke 10:33–34a). It is also possible that the oil was symbolic of the Holy Spirit. In either case, we should not think that there was anything magical or efficacious about the anointing with oil. God is the only one who has healing power.

I think it is both biblical and responsible that the church pray for healing and encourage those who are sick to seek wise medical counsel. This is frequently where balance is missing. Some people appear to believe that if they contact a doctor they would be showing a lack of faith and thus forfeit their opportunity for divine healing. God is omnipotent and we do not limit His healing power by visiting a doctor. Most good physicians I have known admit that they do their best to bring healing through the medical skills they possess, but they cannot bring healing. There is always something that transcends the medical process.

There is a fourth step in this text, which is often overlooked. James indicates that we should confess our sins one to another. We should not take this to mean that there is a direct correlation between sin and a particular illness. Jesus had to correct this mistaken notion among His disciples when they asked about the man born blind (John 9:1–3). The confession of sin points to the need to focus on the more significant issue of spiritual wholeness.

One Sunday morning, while I was pastor in Norfolk, a young lady and her husband asked to meet with me and the spiritual leaders for prayer for a physical problem. We met in my office after church for privacy and intimacy, and I asked several deacons to join us for the prayer time. When the woman arrived, it was not difficult to see that, among other things, she had an eating disorder. Without asking her concerning her particular

prayer request, I suggested that we read James 5 and do whatever it required.

After reading the text, I asked her if there was any area of unconfessed sin that she needed to deal with before we began our prayer time. Unexpectedly, she began to weep. She looked at her husband and then turned her head away. You could see that she was going through an incredible struggle. Painfully, she confessed that she had been sexually abused when she was younger. Though she had been the victim of sin rather than the sinner, the guilt and shame she felt had certainly contributed to the physical problems she was experiencing.

This previous sexual abuse had manifested itself as frigidity in her relationship with her husband. Now she poured out this long buried secret, not knowing how anyone in the room would respond. Her husband reached over to her and enfolded her in love. She realized in that instant that she had married a man who offered her unconditional love. All those years, she had blamed herself for being the victim of sexual abuse. She had been afraid that her husband would hate her if he knew the truth. Instead, his love and forgiveness opened the door for her healing. There was an absolute outpouring of the Holy Spirit in that room. She had received both spiritual and physical healing. She discovered that God was indeed Jehovah Rophe. Her healing process began that day. We then referred her to a good physician who could help reverse some of the damage that she had suffered through her eating disorder and we made her an appointment with our Christian counselor, who helped her to find healing for her damaged psyche.

While I was preaching this series at First Baptist in Dallas, we had the wonderful opportunity to practice James 5. A godly gentleman in our church was dying from cancer that had ravaged his body. He requested that we come to his home, anoint him with oil, and pray for his healing. Nearly twenty men gathered around his bed and poured out their hearts in prayer. It was one of the most worshipful experiences anyone could desire. That gentleman recently received his perfect healing. He went home to be with the Lord. Just before he died, he told me how significant that prayer meeting had been for him and his wife. First, he was convinced that God, in response to our prayers, had prolonged his life, giving him the time he needed to complete several ministry projects. But more importantly, it had enabled him to live in peace with his cancer, knowing that he was in the care of Jehovah Rophe.

There is healing for your deepest pains and disappointment. There is healing for your past. There is victory over addictions. There is both physical and spiritual healing available in Christ. If you have become sidetracked at Marah, bitter in your soul and spirit, feeling that life has been unfair to you, the only way you can go from Marah to Elim and find sweet water is to turn to Jehovah Rophe. Jesus is Jehovah Rophe, almighty to heal.

— 8 —

JEHOVAH NISSI

THE LORD IS MY BANNER

And Moses built an altar and named it

The-LORD-Is-My-Banner;

for he said, "Because the LORD has sworn: The

LORD will have war with

Amalek from generation to generation."

EXODUS 17:15–16, NKJV

There has been a revival of the use of banners in the church today. Colorful banners with the various names of Jesus are often used to accompany some of the great anthems and musicals that focus on Christ. It wasn't long ago that banners were premiered for many Southern Baptists at an annual convention. I recall watching the expression of those around me, many of whom were seeing banners used in worship for the first time. At first, there was mild amusement as they enjoyed the colorful banners. But as the procession continued toward a climax with a beautiful and majestic banner with streamers representing Jesus, tears began to flow. In the years that have followed, many churches have incorporated banners to enhance the visible content of the worship experience. When this series of messages was preached at First Baptist in Dallas, it was accompanied by beautiful banners designed by members of the church.

Why the interest in banners? They certainly add color and visual stimulation to the worship experience. Yet I think one of the reasons for the renewed interest is to be found in the understanding of the name, Jehovah Nissi, the Lord is our Banner.

SETTING THE HISTORICAL CONTEXT

When the children of Israel left Marah, their journey took them through Elim, a place of rest with beautiful palm trees and refreshing water. In due time, their journey necessitated that they leave Elim and travel through the wilderness of Sin, which is between Elim and Sinai. Exodus 16:2 sounds familiar: "And the whole congregation of the sons of Israel grumbled against Moses and Aaron in the wilderness."

The issue of their grumbling again centered around their appetites. Listen to the complaint registered in verse 3: "Would that we had died by the LORD's hand in the land of Egypt, when we sat by the pots of meat, when we ate bread to the full; for you have brought us out into this wilderness to kill this whole assembly with hunger."

In response to their complaints, the Lord made it rain bread and quail from heaven daily to provide food. Yet, with His provision, He put in place a test. The people were to take only enough manna for the needs of the day. Only on the sixth day were they to gather two portions, in preparation for the Sabbath. Once again, the Lord is developing a people who will rely upon Him for their daily needs. It is difficult for us not to think of the prayer that Jesus first taught His disciples when He told them to ask the Lord for their daily bread. Jesus wanted His followers to learn to rely upon the Father daily for their provision. It is imperative that believers of every age grow in their relationship with God so that they trust Him to supply their every need.

In Exodus 17, we find that Israel has journeyed from the wilderness of Sin and camped at Rephidim. Here, once again, their faith is tested by the absence of water. Unfortunately, the people again respond by complaining. "But the people thirsted there for water; and they grumbled against Moses and said, 'Why, now, have you brought us up from Egypt, to kill us and our children and our livestock with thirst?'" (v. 3). Moses cried out to the Lord fearing that the people would take his life. The Lord told him to take his rod and strike the rock so that He could provide water. The place was named Massah and Meribah because the people quarreled and "because they tested the Lord, saying, 'Is the LORD among us, or not'" (17:7).

As we follow this journey, we are astounded by Israel's stubborn unbelief. You would think that they would have learned to trust the Lord and not to test Him. He had miraculously saved them at the Red Sea, He had made bitter water sweet, He had rained food from the skies, and yet they tested Him. Notice, too, that the testing is accompanied by grumbling and complaining. Spiritual unbelief is often detected in one's spirit and attitude. When we fail to see God's hand in our daily affairs and to trust Him for our daily provision, we begin to fret and complain about our difficult circumstances. Like Israel, we need to understand what it means to have the Lord for our Banner.

The truth is, we have not yet discussed the real issue that would test the people's faith at Rephidim. They would soon find that thirst was the least of their worries, because they were about to face the Amalekites. In verse 8, we read: "Then Amalek came and fought against Israel at Rephidim."

RECOGNIZING THE ENEMY

Who were the Amalekites? The Amalekites were the descendants of Amalek, a grandson of Esau, Jacob's brother. In Genesis 36:12 we read, "And Timna was a concubine of Esau's son Eliphaz and she bore Amalek to Eliphaz." Let me remind you of the family intrigue wrapped up in Esau's history. Jacob and Esau were twin sons born to Isaac and Rebekah. Esau was born first, but Jacob was born clutching to Esau's heel. Esau was an outdoors man, a rugged and skillful hunter, and the favorite of his father. Jacob was a peaceful man who was favored by his mother.

The intrigue began when Esau sold Jacob his birthright for a bowl of stew (Gen. 25:27–34). Esau saw no need to preserve a future blessing when he had such a pressing present need. Years later, when their father, Isaac, had grown old and his eyesight had become too dim to see, as he was preparing to pass on the blessing to Esau, his elder son, he first sent him on a mission to hunt for game to prepare for him a savory dish. Rebekah overheard the conversation and encouraged Jacob to deceive his father and steal the blessing. The mother prepared a savory dish and Jacob dressed in Esau's garments and used the skins of the kids as a covering for his hands and the smooth part of his neck. In this way, the nearly blind Isaac was tricked into blessing the younger son (Gen. 27).

The enmity that began on that day persisted generation after generation. Even though the Amalekites were direct descendants of Isaac, they became the hereditary enemy of Israel, a constant prevailing threat to their spiritual and national life. Thus the Amalekites represent the forces of evil who stand in opposition to God's people.

The Strategy of the Enemy

Deuteronomy 25 contains the story of the second giving of the Law. After Israel had failed to enter the Promised Land when God first brought them to the banks of the Jordan, they wandered in the wilderness until the unbelieving generation had died. Now they are poised once again to enter Canaan and Moses reminds them of the various laws that God had set in place for their protection. After reciting the laws, he warns them of the consequences of disobedience. He uses the memory of the Amalekites and their attempt to destroy Israel to insist that the people must do away completely with sin. "'Remember what Amalek did to you along the way when you came out from Egypt, how he met you along the way and attacked among you all the stragglers at your rear when you were faint and weary; and he did not fear God'" (Deut. 25:17–18).

The strategy of Amalek is like that of our adversary, the devil. Peter describes these tactics: "Your adversary, the devil, prowls about like a roaring lion, seeking someone to devour" (1 Pet. 5:8b). Moses tells the people of Israel that when the Lord gives them rest from their enemies, they must completely blot out the memory of Amalek. You cannot strike a truce with Satan.

Centuries after the message recorded in Deuteronomy, Samuel came to King Saul with a commission from Jehovah God to utterly destroy the Amalekites. "Thus says the LORD of hosts, 'I will punish Amalek *for* what he did to Israel, how he set himself against him on the way while he was coming up from Egypt. Now go and strike Amalek and utterly destroy all that he has, and do not spare him'" (1 Sam. 15:2–3a).

When we read such verses we sometimes recoil from the implication of God's command to utterly destroy Amalek, because we do not fully comprehend the strategy of the enemy. The Amalekites represent the forces of evil as they oppose the work of God and the people of God. The goal of Amalek is to utterly destroy the people of God. When there is compromise with sin, sin begins its insidious work to corrupt and ultimately destroy us.

You may remember that King Saul failed to carry out this command and it ultimately led to his own rejection as king and to his death. Ironically, the young man who ultimately bore responsibility for Saul's death was an Amalekite. One whom Saul had foolishly spared later returned to hasten his death.

THE DECEPTIVE POWER OF SIN

The adversary has but one goal and that is to steal, kill, and destroy the work of God in the lives of His people. That is precisely the reason that Jesus clearly articulates the need to destroy the power of sin in our lives. In the Sermon on the Mount, Jesus indicates that if our right eye makes us stumble in the matter of lust and the accompanying sin of adultery, we would be better to tear it out and throw it from our body than to allow it to send us to hell (Matt. 5:28–29). Jesus was not suggesting the mutilation of our bodies, but He was encouraging us to deal radically with sin in our life, and to have a realistic understanding of the work of the adversary and the power of sin.

The adversary is out to destroy you, and you must not deal lightly with the presence of sin in your life. We sometimes quote 1 John 1:9: "If we confess our sins, He is faithful and righteous to forgive us our sins and to cleanse us from all unrighteousness," as if it were little more than a spiritual Band-Aid. We can be tempted to think that sin really doesn't impact our lives and we have this "forgiveness credit card" that lets us sin with impunity. But we forget that sin grieves the heart of Holy God and seeks to destroy our spiritual victory. It is like cancer—once it gains a foothold, it begins to spread its death throughout the body. The only cure for the cancer is to totally obliterate the deadly cells.

A few years ago while on an airplane, I read a fascinating but rather unpleasant story. It had all the qualities of a good mystery. A frantic 9-1-1 call brought the local police to a home. The caller had only been able to communicate that she needed help and that she was being killed. When the police arrived, they found a bloody knife beside her lifeless body on the kitchen floor. Blood was spattered across the room, yet when the police examined the body, they found to their amazement not a single cut or puncture wound. The only evidence on her body was a large mark across her chest and neck.

They then noticed a trail of blood leading into the next room. Following the blood they found a dying boa constrictor.

The woman had apparently raised the snake as a pet. On this particular day, the snake had apparently wrapped itself around the woman as she prepared food in the kitchen. For whatever reason, she had allowed the snake to entwine her body. Once the muscular snake began to constrict itself, the woman had apparently sensed the danger. In a panic, she had grabbed a knife and began to slash away. She managed to mortally wound the snake, but she was killed in the process.

This story is an incredible example of the power of sin in our lives. We often take subtle compromises into our lives like an innocent pet. We think we can handle the snake without any real risk. Although we hear stories about the destruction of other people, we rationalize that they were simply weak. We can handle it! We think we know how far we can go. Thus we deal with sin flippantly and lightly.

ISRAEL GOES TO WAR WITH AMALEK

As we return to the story in Exodus 17, we find that Moses has commissioned Joshua to select men to join him as he goes out to encounter the Amalekites. While Joshua is leading the troops forward, Moses stations himself on the top of a nearby hill with the staff of God in his hand. There is no indication of fear or confusion as Israel faces Amalek, and it is highly unlikely that the Amalekites feared the people of Israel. These wandering people were ill-equipped for battle. They were little more than an inexperienced mob, fleeing captivity. The battle plan appears somewhat unorthodox. Joshua and his men will fight while Moses sits on a hill with the rod of God held aloft. We are told that when the rod was held aloft, Israel prevailed, but when his arms became heavy and he let his arms down, Amalek had the upper hand. Ultimately, Aaron and Hur supported Moses' arms and he was able to keep his arms steady until the setting of the sun. The end result: "So Joshua overwhelmed Amalek and his people with the edge of the sword" (Exod. 17:13).

THE LORD IS MY BANNER

It was not simply Moses' dramatic and visible posture on the hilltop that inspired confidence in his troops; it was the rod of God held aloft that brought them victory. Though the rod was likely nothing more than a shepherd's staff, God had used it as an object lesson to show Moses His power to accomplish His work.

Back in Exodus 4, when God called Moses to lead Israel out of captivity, and Moses objected that no one would believe him or listen to what he had to say, God asked what he had in his hand. It was his shepherd's staff. God then instructed him to throw the staff on the ground, whereupon it became a serpent. The Lord then instructed Moses to take the serpent by the tail and once he did, it again became a staff. This staff was to be used as a sign that the God of Israel had appeared to Moses (Exod. 4:5). When Moses obeyed God and departed for Egypt, he took the staff of God with him (4:20). From this point forward, this simple staff became the rod of God, which Moses used to effect various plagues in Egypt and the striking of the rock that provided water for the thirsting Israelites in the wilderness (Exod. 17:5–6).

It is this same rod that is now called "the Lord is my Banner." This visible symbol was intended to illustrate graphically to all of Israel's warriors that the victory over Amalek belonged to God. Israel could do nothing in themselves to defeat the Amalekites, but under the banner of the Lord, victory was assured.

You might be surprised, as I was, to find a simple staff depicted as a banner. A banner in ancient times was not always a flag, as we think of a banner today. Often it was a bare staff with a shiny metal ornament that would glisten in the sun. In fact, the word translated *banner* means "to glisten."

In Psalm 74:4, the psalmist speaks of the enemy setting up their standards or banners in their camp as a sign of victory. In Psalm 60:4–6, we have a wonderful picture of God's protection and deliverance under the imagery of a banner:

> Thou has given a banner to those who fear Thee,
> That it may be displayed because of the truth,
> That Thy beloved may be delivered,
> Save with Thy right hand, and answer us!

When we understand that Jehovah has become our Banner, we can come under Him for our victory.

This banner in the hand of Moses was a visible image of the protection and the power of God, who would provide the victory over Amalek. The Israelites were to understand that their victory was a miracle provided by Jehovah.

The Serpent on a Pole

One of the most famous banners in the Old Testament is found in the Book of Numbers. While Israel was wandering in the wilderness, they journeyed from Mt. Hor by the way of the Red Sea (21:4). As they traveled, the people became hungry and thirsty and they began to complain against the Lord. But then they faced a danger greater than the lack of food. They were being bitten by poisonous serpents and many of the people began to die. They confessed to Moses their sin against the Lord and he interceded for them before the Lord.

"Then the Lord said to Moses, 'Make a fiery serpent and set it on a standard; and it shall come about, that everyone who is bitten, when he looks at it, he shall live.' And Moses made a bronze serpent and set it on the standard; and it came about, that if a serpent bit any man, when he looked to the bronze serpent, he lived" (21:8–9).

What an image! A serpent on a stick. We know that a mere bronze serpent stuck on a pole has no power to bring healing. The healing was from the Lord. Only He could bring the solution to the problem they faced. They had encountered the fiery serpents because of their disobedience, and their sin had put them in peril. There was no antivenin in those days, no hospitals nearby. The people would surely die unless God intervened. Yet their healing depended upon their obedience to look by faith upon the banner the Lord had provided.

We encounter an interesting reference to this Old Testament banner in John's Gospel, when Nicodemus, a Pharisee and a member of the Sanhedrin, came to visit Jesus at night. He confessed that he believed that Jesus came from God and worked miraculous signs. His inquiry apparently dealt with how a man could enter the Kingdom of God (3:3).

In His response, Jesus referred to the serpent in the wilderness, a story with which Nicodemus would have been very familiar, and He compared this Old Testament event to His coming crucifixion. "'And as Moses lifted up the serpent in the wilderness, even so must the Son of Man be lifted up; that whoever believes may in Him have eternal life'" (3:14–15). When I first understood the implication of this text, I found it somewhat repulsive. How can we compare the crucifixion of Jesus with the lifting up of a bronze serpent on a stick?

Here's the point. Israel needed salvation from the deadly bite of the serpents, and God commanded Moses to put a bronze snake on a staff. Mankind needs to be delivered from the curse of sin, and God placed a sin offering of His own on a staff—His Son, Jesus Christ, who was lifted up on a cross. The apostle Paul explained the transaction this way: "He made Him who knew no sin to be sin on our behalf, that we might become the righteousness of God in Him" (2 Cor. 5:21). Jesus, as our High Priest, did not simply bring a sin offering before the Father; He became the sin offering Himself.

The prophet Isaiah prophesied that the Messiah would become the offering for our sin:

> Surely our griefs He Himself bore,
> And our sorrows He carried;
> Yet we ourselves esteemed Him stricken,
> Smitten of God, and afflicted.
> But He was pierced through for our
>   transgressions,
> He was crushed for our iniquities;
> The chastening for our well-being fell
>   upon him
> And by His scourging we are healed. (Isa. 53:4–5)

While other religions attempt to provide ways to appease God by works of righteousness, Christianity tells us that Jesus Himself was the offering that appeased God's wrath. The transaction that occurred on the cross is not a pleasant thought; the sacrifice was a costly one. Jesus, who from the very beginning of time was fully God, had never been separated from God the Father. But when the penalty of our sin was placed upon Him and He became the sin offering, He was separated from God the Father by our sin. Do you remember the agonizing cry that fell from His lips? "And about the ninth hour Jesus cried out with a loud voice, saying, 'ELI, ELI, LAMA SABACHTHANI?' that is, 'MY GOD, MY GOD, WHY HAST THOU FORSAKEN ME?'" (Matt. 27:46).

Yet the good news is that the cross stands empty today. Death could not contain the Lord. He was raised victorious from the dead to give us victory over sin and death. Do you remember the first sermon that Peter preached in the Book of Acts? "Men of Israel, listen to these words: Jesus the Nazarene, a man attested to you by God with miracles and wonders and signs which God performed through Him in your midst, just as you yourselves know—this Man, delivered up by the predetermined plan and foreknowledge of God, you nailed to a cross by the hands of godless men and put Him to death. And God raised Him up again, putting an end to the agony of death, since it was impossible for Him to be held in its power" (Acts 2:22–24). Jesus is the Banner of Jehovah, who provides forgiveness of sin and grants eternal life.

STANDING UNDER THE BANNER OF THE LORD

The first issue you must resolve is whether Jesus has become your Jehovah Nissi in terms of your relationship to God. He was lifted up on the cross as the sacrifice for sin, but you must respond by faith even as Israel had to look upon the bronze serpent by faith. John says, "But as many as received Him, to them He gave the right to become children of God, even to those who believe in His name" (John 1:12). If you have never invited

Him to come into your life, why don't you pause and do that right now. You can simply tell Him that you are a sinner and need His forgiveness. Then in your own words invite Him to come into your life, forgive your sins, and be your personal Savior.

If you have already experienced Jesus as your Savior, you may need to experience Him as the one who gives you daily victory over sin. When Israel came to the Red Sea, they were commanded to stand still and see the salvation of the Lord, but when they came against Amalek, they were told to go to battle under the banner of the Lord. Remember, Amalek represents the forces of sin, which stand opposed to God and His people in every age. When Paul exhorts Christians to put on the whole armor of God, he also reminds them that "our struggle is not against flesh and blood, but against the rulers, against the powers, against the world forces of this darkness, against the spiritual forces of wickedness in the heavenly places" (Eph. 6:12).

We are called to "fight the good fight of faith." To do so we must put on the whole armor of God, living in continual confession and repentance, walking daily with God, and standing under the Banner of Jehovah Nissi. You can be assured that you have spiritual victory. Paul can state with firm assurance: "But in all these things we overwhelmingly conquer through Him who loved us" (Rom. 8:37). You can live the victorious Christian life. Jesus is your Jehovah Nissi.

9

JEHOVAH MEKADESH

THE LORD WHO SANCTIFIES YOU

"You shall keep My statutes, and practice them;

I am the LORD who sanctifies you."

LEVITICUS 20:8

The words to an old spiritual song declare, "Lord, I want to be a Christian in my heart . . . Lord, I want to be more holy . . ." We don't hear much about holiness today. Yet God commands Israel: "For I am the LORD your God. Consecrate yourselves therefore, and be holy; for I am holy" (Lev. 11:44a). Holiness is not an idea confined to a few obscure Old Testament passages. Peter quotes Leviticus 11:44 as he calls his readers to a radical lifestyle that befits their calling. He tells them that they can no longer be conformed to the former lusts which marked their pre-conversion lifestyles: "but like the Holy One who called you, be holy yourselves also in all your behavior; because it is written, 'YOU SHALL BE HOLY, FOR I AM HOLY'" (1 Pet. 1:15–16).

Few people get excited about reading the Book of Leviticus. In fact, many Christians begin their annual pilgrimage to read through the Bible with great resolve only to flounder when they get to Leviticus. If you have struggled to find meaning in this great Old Testament book, I hope this chapter will not only give you a greater love for the truth and spiritual richness that pervades Leviticus, but that it will help you reflect upon the powerful name of *Jehovah Mekadesh.*

REMEMBER THE PROGRESSION

The name Jehovah Mekadesh, the God who sanctifies, is first found in Leviticus 20:8. Though we should be careful not to read too much into the order in which the names of God are revealed, occasionally there are some interesting insights that can be gained by paying attention to sequence. The order of revelation sometimes shows both purpose and progression. In that vein, it is noteworthy that the name Jehovah Mekadesh appears for the first time here in the Book of Leviticus. God continues to reveal more of Himself to His people as they are able to comprehend His truth. Have you not found it to be true that God unveils more of His majesty as we learn more about Him?

Thus far, we have learned about Elohim, the Creator, who is almighty over all the earth. We then learned that He is Adonai, the Lord and Master of all, and that we are to live in joyful submission to Him. In the name El Elyon, we discovered the wonderful truth that God, as the Possessor of heaven and earth, can meet our every need. We learned that, as El Shaddai, He is God Almighty to nourish, providing all of our needs. In the name Jehovah (Yahweh), we found that He is the absolutely self-existent One, who established a covenant with His people to allow them to know Him in personal relationship. In Jehovah Jireh we found our Provider, who desires to release His blessings in our life. As Israel journeyed through the wilderness they discovered God to be Jehovah Rophe, the God who turns the bitter to sweet, providing healing for life. Jehovah Nissi is our Banner for victorious living.

At this point in the life of the nation, Israel is a redeemed people. They have been taken from Egyptian captivity and are being prepared to inhabit the Promised Land. What was Israel to be like in their relationship to God? How are they supposed to live? How will they maintain their distinctive qualities as a people related to God when they settle in a land inhabited by pagan nations who do not know God? This question is as relevant today as it was thousands of years ago.

To answer such questions, God inspired Moses to write the Book of Leviticus. It has been called the Book of Life. It is indeed about the walk and worship of the redeemed people. It was not until the redemption of the Exodus had been accomplished that Israel could begin to understand and submit themselves to the sanctifying work of a holy God.

The name Jehovah Mekadesh means the God who sanctifies. Interestingly, this is not the first biblical reference to the concept of sanctification. In Genesis 2:3 we read: "Then God blessed the seventh day and sanctified it, because in it He rested from all His work which God had created and made." This day was set apart or "sanctified" from the other days so that we could worship the Creator with our entire attention. Soon after creation, sin entered into this garden experience. After the fall, the word *sanctify* does not occur again until Exodus 13:2 where God tells Israel to sanctify all of their firstborn. It was only after the redemption experience of the Exodus that sanctification could be resumed in the life of Israel.

The Book of Leviticus answers practical questions about the walk of God's people, so we should not be surprised that the title Jehovah Mekadesh is repeated six times in two chapters. Like Israel, we have been set apart as a holy people. Sanctification suggests that we should be like God in our purity and be set apart unto Him for service. Let's look at this process as we study this name.

HOLINESS EXPRESSES THE NATURE OF GOD

The term *sanctify* appears frequently in the Old Testament, occurring about seven hundred times in various forms. The word can also be translated as "to dedicate," "to consecrate," or "to hallow." In our primary text, we will notice that the command for Israel to consecrate themselves is followed by the explanation that their God is holy and the God who sanctifies. "'You shall consecrate yourselves therefore and be holy, for I am the LORD your God. And you shall keep My statutes and practice them; I am the LORD [Jehovah Mekadesh] who sanctifies you" (Lev. 20:7–8). If you look at the immediate context, you will find prohibitions against turning to mediums and spiritists, cursing one's parents, and various sexual sins. The positive antidote against such defiling behavior is to keep the statutes of God and to practice them in everyday life.

The name Jehovah Mekadesh is often overlooked because it is not translated in the English Bible in this recognizable form. Yet there is no other name for God that more adequately expresses His nature and the requirements He places on His people.

In 1 Samuel 2:1–2, we read the beautiful prayer of Hannah after she had dedicated Samuel to the service of the Lord:

> Then Hannah prayed and said,
> "My heart exults in the LORD;
> My horn is exalted in the LORD,
> My mouth speaks boldly against my enemies,
> Because I rejoice in Thy salvation.
> There is no one holy like the LORD,
> Indeed, there is no one beside Thee,
> Nor is there any rock like our God."

Hannah declares that God by His very nature is holy. If we are going to understand and declare the nature of God, we must begin by understanding that He is holy. Hannah also declares that God's holiness sets Him apart from all other gods. He alone is God. This affirmation of the uniqueness of God is critical in our pluralistic society, which is moving us toward polytheism, the belief in the existence of many gods.

God's essential attribute is His holiness. Perhaps you thought that *love* would be God's primary attribute. Certainly, John declares that God is love. "And we have come to know and have believed the love which God has for us. God is love, and the one who abides in love abides in God, and God abides in him"

(1 John 4:16). Or we could point to John 3:16, which declares that God's great love prompted Him to send His only begotten Son for our redemption. Yet, if you follow John's argument, you will find that the redeeming love of God was to make us fit for His holy presence. Man, in his sin, has fallen short of the glory of God and has broken his relationship with the Holy God. Thus we cannot approach Him in our own flesh. But God, out of His love, redeemed us so that we could have a relationship with Him.

An old Scottish theologian, Nathan Stone, wrote concerning holiness: "It is the balance . . . of all the attributes of Deity."[1] He further argues that power without holiness would degenerate into cruelty. Omniscience without holiness would become craft. Justice without holiness would degenerate into revenge. Goodness without holiness would be passionate and intemperate fondness, doing mischief rather than accomplishing good. We could add that love without holiness would become little more than anemic sentimentality; and freedom without holiness, mere license. *It is the holiness of God that constitutes the perfection of all His attributes.*

It was a vision of God's holiness that transformed Isaiah's life and led to his calling as a powerful spokesman for God. When you read the first chapters of Isaiah you discover that he was praying for revival and spiritual renewal in a bankrupt nation. As he was praying in the temple, He saw the Lord sitting on a throne, lofty and exalted. He saw the seraphim and heard them crying out to one another: "Holy, Holy, Holy, is the LORD of hosts, / The whole earth is full of His glory" (Isa. 6:3). The prophet then felt the foundations tremble as the temple filled with smoke. His response to his encounter with a holy God was, "Woe is me, for I am ruined! / Because I am a man of unclean lips, / and I live among a people of unclean lips; / For my eyes have seen the King, the LORD of hosts" (6:5).

❧

When Isaiah encountered the Holy God, he recognized his own sinfulness. He realized that not only are the people of the nation sinful, but he the prophet was a man of unclean lips. For a man whose profession called for him to speak on behalf of a holy God, the confession that his lips were unclean strikes at the very core of his being. "Then one of the seraphim flew to me, with a burning coal in his hand which he had taken from the altar with tongs. And he touched my mouth with it and said, 'Behold, this has touched your lips; and your iniquity is taken away, and your sin is forgiven'" (6:6–7). The prophet is cleansed by a holy God and it is then that he cries out to God to send him. He is now prepared for service. He is set apart by the God who sanctifies.

It is not insignificant that God's Spirit is referred to as the *Holy* Spirit. That is not simply a title for the third person of the Trinity; it is a clear recognition that God is a holy God—and when He expresses Himself as Spirit, He is a holy Spirit. David recognized this. In Psalm 51:11, he cried out: "Do not cast me away from Thy presence, / And do not take Thy Holy Spirit from me."

The awe-inspiring circumstances surrounding the giving of the law at Mount Sinai were intended to express the holiness of Jehovah. And when we read the final book of the Bible, we are told that the four living creatures will spend eternity praising God. Their song will be, "Holy, Holy, Holy, is the Lord God, the Almighty, who was and who is and who is to come." The consistent theme of Scripture is that holiness characterizes the nature of our God.

The Holiness of God Demands Our Separation from Sin

The fact that God is holy means that those who would relate to Him must be cleansed of their sin. Yet, because we have a sin nature, we know that we cannot of ourselves live a holy existence. Sanctified holiness means that we must come to participate in the nature of God Himself.

In the first few verses of Leviticus 18, the Lord instructs Moses to tell His people: "I am the LORD your God. You shall not do what is done in the land of Egypt where you lived, nor are you to do what is done in the land of Canaan where I am bringing you; you shall not walk in their statutes. You are to perform My judgments and keep My statutes, to live in accord with them; I am the LORD your God" (Lev. 18:2–5). In Egypt and Canaan, Israel had lived among people who did not live by God's standards or worship Him as God. Yet Israel was admonished not to copy the standards of the world, that they must be set apart (sanctified) to follow the standards that were given by God and which reflected His holy nature.

In Leviticus 19, God again challenges Israel to be holy because He is holy. Note, for example, verses 2 and 3: "You shall be holy, for I the LORD your God am holy. Every one of you shall reverence his mother and his father, and you shall keep My sabbaths; I am the LORD your God." As you read the rest of chapter 19, you will find instruction concerning such matters as reverencing one's mother and father, respecting older persons, keeping the sabbath, laws for harvesting (with particular concern for leaving some of the grain for the unfortunate), how those who work for you should be treated, using just weights and measures, and avoiding mediums and spiritists. These are a few of the matters that are to be part of Israel's behavior, and each is related to the holy character of God. For example, Israel was called to leave a portion of the harvest for the poor and the stranger, because such behavior reflected the God they served. He is a God who cares for the poor and the stranger, and His people must therefore do the same.

In like manner, as Christians we are called to give and to share, because that is the nature of God, who lives in us. If you look at history you will find that Christians in every generation have started hospitals, care facilities for the aging, and benevolent organizations. Why? Is it because we are such good or generous people? No! It is because such behavior reflects the God we serve. You don't see a historical record of atheists or humanists caring for the needy with the passion that Christians have. Why? Because human nature unaided by God is basically selfish and unconcerned. We care because God cares through us.

The challenges Israel faced as they settled in a pagan culture are not dissimilar to those we face today. We are in moral quicksand in our society. There is much debate and confusion about moral values. Some people claim that there are no moral absolutes. Many are certainly living as though moral values are all personally determined. Such a position will ultimately lead to moral confusion and will become destructive in daily life. No society can survive without established values to guide daily living.

Many people seem to think that moral values should be established by the community at large, perhaps by consensus or democratic vote. Thus, if a society changes its mind about issues such as abortion or euthanasia, then they have every right to change the laws and alter the moral values by which we live. A system that bases moral values on consensus has no absolutes. Values change at the whim of the public. If we follow the implications of such a system to their logical ends, no one would have the right to be outraged about the treatment of the Jews by Adolf Hitler, because the consensus feeling at the time seemed to support Hitler's notion that the Jews could be annihilated as non-persons. Only in a society based on absolute values about the worth of every human being can such atrocities be avoided.

Moral values cannot be based on personal whims or the fickle opinions of an ever-changing majority. To endure, they must be anchored in an unchanging reality. Moral and ethical values are based on the character of Holy God. That's why the Ten Commandments are as essential today as they were thousands of years ago. They reflect the holy and unchanging nature of the God who created us and who desires for us to experience a full and productive life in Him.

When God reveals that He is Jehovah Mekadesh, the God who sanctifies, He declares that the people He has redeemed will separate themselves from sin because they bear His nature. To live according to the standards of the world would profane His holy name.

You may be asking how you can live a holy life that would honor His name. Paul deals with that very issue in Romans 7:14–8:39. He first confesses his own struggle to obey God's perfect law when his flesh waged war against the desire of his heart. He cries out, "Wretched man that I am! Who will set me free from the body of this death?" (Rom. 7:24). Paul then answers his own cry with thanksgiving that the law of the Spirit of Christ had set him free from the law of sin and death. Those who belong to Jesus Christ have the Spirit of Christ indwelling them (8:9). "But if the Spirit of Him who raised Jesus from the dead dwells in you, He who raised Christ Jesus from the dead will also give life to your mortal bodies through His Spirit who indwells you" (8:11).

Isn't it wonderful news that we have the Holy Spirit of God indwelling us, creating in us His own nature so that we can obey His law and live victoriously over sin? After we are born again, God produces in us His nature and thus His character flows from us and can be described as the fruit of the Spirit (Gal. 5:22–24).

HOLINESS MEANS OUR SEPARATION
FOR SERVICE

Israel's separation from sin was for the positive purpose of being a fitting vessel for God's service. Some Bible teachers debate whether holiness means purity from sin or separation for service. The answer is simple: it is both. These two matters are closely related. Holiness means our separation *from* so that we can be separated *to*. We cannot effectively serve a holy God until there is purity in our lives.

The sabbath was a day that was to be sanctified, or set apart for God. The tabernacle, the temple, and the vessels in that temple, were holy in that they were set apart for God's service. These vessels and implements of worship were not only kept pure; they were to be used only in the service of Holy God.

The apostle Paul establishes this same principle in calling the believers in Rome to service. He declares that believers are dead to sin and alive to God. This leads him to the logical conclusion stated in Romans 6:12–13: "Therefore do not let sin reign in your mortal body that you should obey its lusts, and do not go on presenting the members of your body to sin as instruments of unrighteousness; but present yourselves to God as those alive from the dead, and your members as instruments of righteousness to God."

We are saved and cleansed from sin so that we can serve the living God. Nothing should excite us more than the privilege of being the pure instruments through which God accomplishes His work on earth. I am always amazed that some people who call themselves Christians have no desire to serve God through the use of their time, talents, and spiritual gifts. They treat Christianity as a spectator sport, as if others are called to serve

them. When we understand this beautiful name, Jehovah Mekadesh, it should birth in us the passion to be set apart for service. We should be asking how we can use the members of our body as instruments of righteousness. Sanctification should impact our conversations, our business transactions, our relationships, our activities in the community and in our local church, and our study of God's Word.

APPLYING WHAT WE HAVE LEARNED

If we truly grasp the truth of God's holiness, it will radically change our view of sin. Among many Christians today, there seems to be little remorse for the sin in their lives. They treat 1 John 1:9 (the promise that we can confess our sin and be cleansed from unrighteousness) like a spiritual Band-Aid, claiming God's forgiveness without any clear intention of turning away from continued sin. Such an attitude neglects the great truth of repentance. We lose our godly sorrow over sin when we lose sight of the holy nature of God.

Another trap is seeking to justify our sin by measuring ourselves against others whom we deem to be worse than we are. It's like the student who feels good about receiving a *C* on a test because others in the room did worse. When I was pastor, it was not unusual to hear someone say, "Well, pastor, you stepped on my toes today. I'm going to have to start wearing steel-toed shoes to church." What they meant was that the Holy Spirit was dealing with their pet area of sin, but they had no intention of repenting and turning from that sin. They had little remorse and no sense of repentance, because they had little understanding that all sin must be measured against the holiness of God. Our sin grieves God's Spirit because His Spirit, who indwells us, is holy.

A clear understanding of holiness can be an aid to evangelism. When people understand that the standard by which we will be judged is the holiness of God, they will cry out for mercy. They will understand that they can never measure up to the standard of a holy God. The point of redemption is that God must redeem mankind to fit us to stand in His presence. His love for us is so great that He took upon Himself the penalty of our sin so that we might become the righteousness of God in Christ (2 Cor. 5:21). It is with this understanding that Paul declares that we must be ambassadors for Christ, begging people to be reconciled to Holy God.

How do we grow in a holy lifestyle? Let me give you a few practical suggestions from 1 Peter. In chapter 1, Peter reviews the wonderful blessings that we have in Christ Jesus. Based on these wonderful blessings, Peter issues several imperatives: Gird your minds for action. Keep sober in spirit. Fix your hope completely on the grace to be brought to you at the revelation of Jesus Christ. Do not be conformed to your former lusts. Be holy like the Holy One who called you.

In these imperatives and in the chapter that follows, Peter gives us several practical steps to holy living:

Step 1: Prepare your mind for activity. We must come to realize that our mind ultimately controls our actions. If we allow impure thoughts to dominate our minds, they will ultimately lead us to impure actions. We must fill our minds and thoughts with God's Word. Paul gives sound advice concerning our minds in Philippians 4:8: "Finally, brethren, whatever is true, whatever is honorable, whatever is right, whatever is pure, whatever is lovely, whatever is of good repute, if there is any excellence and if anything worthy of praise, let your mind dwell on these things."

Step 2: Put aside those things that quench your appetite for God's Word. Here's the way Peter states it: "Therefore, putting aside all malice and all guile and hypocrisy and envy and all slander . . . long for the pure milk of the word" (1 Pet. 2:1–2). The image of putting off the old man is a frequent one in the New Testament. We must intentionally choose not to sin. We must put aside these sinful attitudes and thoughts, for they war against our holiness.

Step 3: Develop an appetite for the Word of God. "Long for the pure milk of the word, that by it you may grow in respect to salvation" (1 Pet. 2:2). You cannot live holy and live apart from the Bible. The Christian needs both personal and corporate Bible study in order to provide a balanced diet. When personal Bible study is complemented by doctrinally sound teaching through the church, we have the checks and balances necessary to allow the Spirit to speak clearly. We all need a church home that places equal emphasis on corporate worship and small-group Bible study. In 1 Peter 1:22, Peter emphasizes the truth that we have purified our souls for the sincere love of the brethren. Holiness is both a personal and a corporate issue. If you have not found a strong Bible-teaching church, make that a priority. If you have such a church, but you have neglected personal Bible study, you must develop that personal discipline if you are to grow in holiness.

As a growing Christian, you will find that one of the most precious names you will call out in prayer is Jehovah Mekadesh.

Lord, sanctify us. Keep us free from the sin that desires only to destroy us. Lord, set us apart for service to You. Use us today, Lord. Thank You that You allow us to be vessels through whom You work.

1. Nathan Stone, *Names of God* (Chicago: Moody Press, 1944), 99.

10

JEHOVAH SHALOM

THE LORD IS PEACE

So Gideon built an altar there to the LORD, and

called it The-LORD-Is-Peace.

JUDGES 6:24, NKJV

When the angelic messengers declared the coming of the Lord in human flesh, they declared:

> "Glory to God in the highest,
> And on earth peace among men with whom
>   He is pleased." (Luke 2:14)

The coming of Jesus brought about the possibility of peace. The Hebrew word *shalom,* in the compound name for God in this chapter, is translated "peace," but it means much more than the cessation of violence and hostility. There is a considerable difference between peace and a truce. It is glorious good news that Jehovah is peace.

As the twentieth century drew to a close, we were continually reminded that earthly peace has not yet become reality, and what little peace we have is fragile at best. Even after an end to the war in Bosnia and Kosovo, NATO forces remain deployed in numerous hot spots around the world. Political unrest in Indonesia threatens to boil over at any time, and the latest outbreak of violence between the Palestinians and Israelis reminds us of their deep-seated and longstanding enmity toward one another.

What about peace in our churches, our communities, our homes, and our hearts? The tragedy in Littleton, Colorado, shook our world as few recent incidents have shaken us. We find it incomprehensible that two teenagers could be so angry or evil that they could plot the deaths of hundreds of their fellow students and ultimately kill 13 of them—and themselves. How could the peace of this small upper-middle-class community be shattered so decisively and swiftly? The increasing number of psychological counselors and clinics in our country shows how fragile peace is in many of our families. Yet we earnestly desire peace. *Jehovah Shalom* tells us that peace can become reality.

This name is first used in the sixth chapter of Judges. At this point in Israel's history, we are nearly two hundred years removed from the revelation of God as Jehovah Mekadesh, the God who sanctifies. Moses and Joshua have passed off the scene. The hope of the Promised Land had now been realized, and the land had been divided among the tribes of Israel. Yet, even though they had taken the land, there was no unity among the people. Let's look briefly at the characteristics of that day so that we might better understand the name "The Lord is Peace."

THE PERIOD OF THE JUDGES

Israel's early years in Canaan bear great similarity to the conditions we see in the world today. There was no central worship. This period was characterized as a time when every man did what was right in his own eyes. They believed they were a law unto themselves. The people of Israel, who had been set apart as a holy people unto God, had lost the sense of being a special people and their standards had been compromised.

Some of the people were tempted to turn to the gods of the people around them. These gods of polytheism were fertility gods, gods of sun and moon and harvest. When the wandering Israelites saw the fertile farms of their pagan neighbors, they were tempted to turn to their gods for help. No doubt they continued to remember the God of Israel, but they were willing to accommodate themselves to the gods of polytheism. Their whole existence revolved around possessing the land and accumulating all they could. Short-term goals became the focus of their lives. We can see why they were so attracted to the materialistic gods of the heathen. Without a sense of mission, there was no unity and no purpose among the people of Israel. Simply put, they had failed to realize their destiny as the people of God, a unique people set apart for His purpose and His service. Without spiritual vision and purpose, they fell prey to the appetites and desires of the flesh and became like the pagan culture in which they lived.

The similarities to our own nation are so obvious that we shouldn't miss them. Our country was once populated with those seeking religious and political freedom. Our founders had a passion to be one nation under God, and God's blessings were poured out upon our nation. Yet, in our generation, it seems that we have taken God's blessings for granted, and in the process we have begun to bow down to the gods of materialism. We have lost our moral anchor and we have seen the resulting anarchy and violence that haunts our inner cities, our high schools, and our homes.

When you read the Book of Judges, you will notice a cyclical pattern, a recurring sequence of sin, followed by punishment, followed by a season of repentance and deliverance. The deliverer was usually an anointed judge or military leader provided by the sovereign hand of God. The judge would bring deliverance and there would be spiritual renewal for a short period of time. Then the cycle of sin and punishment would be repeated. When Israel took God's blessings for granted, they began to sin, and their sin resulted in a loss of God's power and provision in their lives. Then, in their spiritual poverty, they would once again cry out to God, and in His mercy He would send another deliverer. Unfortunately, each time the cycle was repeated, it became more severe.

Ultimately, Israel lost the fruit of their land and labor. They sank into virtual slavery inside the Promised Land, this bountiful land that had been given for Israel's provision. Remember, Canaan had been described as a land flowing with milk and honey. When the Israelite spies had first visited the valley of Eshcol, they had cut down a single cluster of grapes and carried it on a pole between two men (Num. 13:23). Now, however, the people were living an impoverished existence in a land of plenty. Without obedience to God, Israel had no right to the land, and one heathen nation after another swept over the land, reaping what Israel had sown.

Perhaps you are thinking that this story sounds remarkably like your own spiritual pilgrimage. You know that you have been saved; you have been delivered from Egypt and you occupy the Promised Land of salvation. Yet you find yourself going through endless cycles of rebellion and loss of blessing, followed by repentance and spiritual deliverance. You wonder if there will ever be an end to the cycles of rebellion and defeat. If you know the consequences of disobedience, why do you repeat these self-defeating behavior patterns?

One day while I was playing golf with a deacon friend in a former pastorate, we began to discuss some of the personal challenges he was facing. He was struggling in his business and his marriage. Finally, I posed a simple question to help him to focus on more positive times in his life. "Tell me about the best times in your marriage and life." He thought about my question for a few minutes and then responded, "Without doubt, the greatest times I have experienced in my personal life have been when I was walking in obedience to the Word of God."

At the moment he gave me that response, he was actually in a period of rebellion. He came to understand that his own personal rebellion had caused the problems he was now facing. Yet his stubborn will kept him from repentance and deliverance.

THE CONQUERING MIDIANITES

For our study of the name Jehovah Shalom, we will pick up the story of Israel's rebellion in Judges 6:

Then the sons of Israel did what was evil in the sight of the LORD; and the LORD gave them into the hands of Midian seven years. And the power of Midian prevailed against Israel. Because of Midian the sons of Israel made for themselves the dens which were in the mountains and the caves and the strongholds. For it was when Israel had sown, that the Midianites would come up with the Amalekites and the sons of the east and go against them. So they would camp against them and destroy the produce of the earth as far as Gaza, and leave no sustenance in Israel as well as no sheep, ox, or donkey. For they would come up with their livestock and their tents, they would come in like locusts for number, both they and their camels were innumerable; and they came into the land to devastate it. So Israel was brought very low because of Midian, and the sons of Israel cried to the LORD. (vv. 1–6)

It's not a very pleasant picture. The children of Israel would plant their crops and the Lord would provide an abundance, but before they could harvest the fields, the Midianites and Amalekites would bring devastation. While destroying the fields, they would steal the livestock. The text indicates that they left no sustenance for Israel and that consequently the Israelites were brought very low. They were devastated and humiliated.

Gideon, God's Deliverer

In verse 7, we begin the second phase in the cycle. We are told that Israel cried out to the Lord because of the attack of the Midianites. The Lord responded by sending a prophet who reminded them

that God had delivered them from the slavery of Egypt and had disposed of the nations, giving Israel the land of promise. They, on the other hand, had not obeyed God's command concerning total allegiance to Him. They had feared the gods of the Amorites.

Nevertheless, God in His infinite mercy was prepared to deliver them once again. When God is about to work in human affairs, He seeks first a human instrument through whom He will bring deliverance. With no fanfare, we are told that the angel of the Lord sat under an oak tree as Gideon, the son of Joash, was beating out wheat to save it from the Midianites (6:11). It has always fascinated me that God calls out ordinary people like us while we are being faithful in the rather mundane affairs of everyday life. As we discuss the text, you will notice that Gideon himself questioned whether he was qualified to accomplish anything of significance for God. Let's look at the dialogue between Gideon and the messenger of the Lord.

"And the angel of the LORD appeared to him and said to him, 'The LORD is with you, O valiant warrior.' Then Gideon said to him, 'O my lord, if the LORD is with us, why then has all this happened to us? And where are all His miracles which our fathers told us about, saying, "Did not the LORD bring us up from Egypt?" But now the LORD has abandoned us and given us into the hand of Midian'" (vv. 12–13).

Repeatedly in Scripture, we find this classic confrontation between the call of God and the reluctance of man to step out in faithful obedience. You may think back to the call of Moses at the burning bush. How can man, who is a created being, say to the Creator, "I am unwilling to fulfill the task for which you have created and called me?"

Actually, in this passage in Judges, before Gideon doubts his own suitability to accomplish the deliverance of Israel, he appears

to call into question the presence and power of the Lord. Gideon wants to know why Israel is experiencing so many disasters if God is on their side. His thinking is simple. If God is with them, the Midianites should not be pillaging their fields. The people of Israel should not be living like animals in caves. He is correct in thinking that it is incongruous for the people of God to be living in such defeat and abject poverty, but he is wrong to conclude that their situation points to the weakness of God.

His second question is similar to the first. *Where are the miracles?* The people of Israel often rehearsed the story of God's redemption and provision. They knew that He had delivered Israel from bondage in Egypt and miraculously saved them at the Red Sea. The stories of God's provision during the wilderness wanderings would have been well known. Therefore, the question appears reasonable to Gideon. Why are we not experiencing God's provision in our day? Although the angel does not immediately answer Gideon's questions, the answers become apparent as the story unfolds.

These two questions may have frequently come to your mind in relationship to your own spiritual life, or your own church. You may be asking where is God's presence and His provision in my own life. This story and the name Jehovah Shalom should give you wonderful good news about God's desire to reveal Himself to you in His sufficiency.

Go . . . Have I Not Sent You?

The Lord's response to Gideon's question is a commission to deliver Israel. "And the LORD looked at him and said, 'Go in this your strength and deliver Israel from the hand of Midian. Have I not sent you?'" (6:14). I find it exciting and challenging to think that God would use the same man who was questioning His provision and presence to be the deliverer through whom

He would reveal His supernatural activity. All the Lord needs is a yielded vessel. When God tells Gideon to go in his strength, it is a divine affirmation that Gideon is capable of doing whatever God calls him to do. We have the same affirmation from God today when He calls us to serve Him by talking to our neighbor or ministering to a friend or teaching a class.

It is at this point that Gideon attempts a second strategic end run. Rather than questioning God's presence or power, he questions his own suitability. These questions sound much more pious and humble. "And he said to Him, 'O Lord, how shall I deliver Israel? Behold, my family is the least in Manasseh, and I am the youngest in my father's house'" (v. 15). Sound familiar? Do you remember the excuses Moses gave? "Who am I to go?" "I'm not a good speaker." We need to remember that all of our excuses are simply that—excuses. When we attempt to question our suitability for any God-given task, we are actually questioning God's choice of us and His ability to use us as He chooses. The Lord's answer to Gideon is reassuring, but firm: "Surely I will be with you, and you shall defeat Midian as one man" (v. 16). When God sends us, He has already assured us that He will be with us and give us the power to accomplish the assigned mission.

Most people who know the story of Gideon remember that he requested a sign from the Lord. Truth is, he asked for several signs. Gideon asked the angel not to leave until he could return with an offering that he will lay out before the angel. He requested a sign to prove to himself that this was truly a messenger from God. When Gideon returned with the offering, the angel instructed him to lay the offering on the rock before him. The angel took the staff that was in his hand and touched the meat and the unleavened bread and fire sprang forth from the rock, consuming the offering.

The next line from the mouth of Gideon may be one of the great understatements of Scripture. "When Gideon saw that he was the angel of the LORD, he said, 'Alas, O Lord GOD! For now I have seen the angel of the LORD face to face'" (v. 22). You may be thinking, What was his first clue? Could it have been the consuming fire that leaped from the rock?

We shouldn't make light of Gideon's perception that this was a messenger from God. Some of us might have missed or, at least dismissed, what Gideon saw. Perhaps God doesn't speak to us in such a dramatic manner, but He continually gives us clear evidence of His presence. When we miss the obvious sign of His presence, we are equally likely to ignore His call to serve Him. Perhaps we see a need or an opportunity in our church or our community. We have the deep impression that something needs to be done to resolve this glaring need. A Christian friend encourages us to take advantage of this opportunity, assuring us that we are the person for the task. Yet we quickly dismiss it as someone else's responsibility, claiming we are not qualified or we are too busy thrashing out wheat. Could it be that we just ignored the fire that leaped from the rock?

The Lord Is Peace

Gideon's response is one of holy fear. He realized that he stood in the presence of a messenger from Holy God. The Hebrew person knew that mortal man could not stand in the presence of Holy God and live. The messenger first assured him that he would not die. "And the LORD said to him, 'Peace to you, do not fear; you shall not die.'" In grateful response, Gideon built an altar in that place and named the altar "The LORD is Peace."

Our English word *peace* translates to the Hebrew *shalom*. You might be wondering what shalom means. It is one of the most

significant terms in the Old Testament. When you visit the Holy Land today, you will hear the word *shalom* frequently, both as a greeting when you meet someone, or as a blessing when you depart.

The word can be translated in several different ways. It can mean "whole," in the sense of "complete." In Deuteronomy, for example, we read: "You shall build the altar of the LORD your God of uncut stones; and you shall offer on it burnt offerings to the LORD your God." The word translated "uncut," referring to a whole or complete stone, is the Hebrew word *shalom*. In 1 Kings 9:25, the same word is translated as "finished." The reference is to the completion of the temple. In Genesis 15:16, Moses uses the word *shalom* when he states that the iniquity of the Amorites was not yet complete or full.

When *shalom* is used in relationship to one's physical being it can be translated as "well" or "wholeness." There are approximately twenty instances in the Bible where *shalom* is translated as "perfect." One of my favorites is 1 Chronicles 29:19 where David prays that God might give his son Solomon a perfect heart. "And give to my son Solomon a perfect heart to keep Thy commandments, Thy testimonies, and Thy statutes, and to do them all, and to build the temple, for which I have made provision." In 1 Kings 8, we have the beautiful prayer of dedication offered to God by Solomon after the temple was completed. After the prayer, Solomon stood to his feet and blessed all the assembly of Israel. First he blesses God for His faithfulness in fulfilling His promises and then he prays for His continued presence and blessing so that all the people of the earth may know that the Lord is God. He ends the blessing with a challenge to Israel: "'Let your heart therefore be wholly devoted to the LORD our God, to walk in His statutes and to keep His commandments, as at this day'" (1 Kings 8:61). Solomon prays that the people of Israel will have a *shalom*, a wholly devoted heart, even as he had experienced through the prayer of his father, David.

The fundamental idea behind the word *shalom* is wholeness in one's relationship with God. *Shalom* defines a harmony of relationship based upon the completion of a transaction, the giving of satisfaction. It does not mean that we simply have a truce, where outward conflict disappears but inner turmoil remains. It is not merely an uneasy cease-fire! In that sense, it is appropriate that *shalom* is translated some 170 times in our English Bible as *peace*.

Shalom expresses the deepest need and desire of the human heart. In our experience, it means a sense of contentment, a freedom from guilt, and a satisfaction with life itself. There is, of course, a requirement. It means that we must have a pure heart before God and live in obedience with His Word and His plan.

A Final Look at Gideon's Questions

Do you remember the two questions asked by Gideon? If God is for us, why are we so afflicted? Where are all the miracles? The answers to these questions are found in the revelation that Jehovah is peace. The people of Israel had expected that they would experience peace once they had been delivered from Egypt and the wilderness wandering and had inhabited the Promised Land. The people of Israel were in the Promised Land but outside the will of God. They had neglected God and ignored His statutes. They were not focused on their unique calling to be about His mission. They didn't understand that peace was not to be found in a physical location, but only in relationship with their creator.

People today make the same mistake when they are empty inside and struggling with their circumstances. They often think that they will have peace if they could move to another location or if they were married to a different person or had a different job. They believe that peace will come when they change the outward circumstances of their life. Like Gideon, they are crying out, "If you are with me, why is my life such a mess?" But we will never know God's peace until we are reconciled with our Creator and live according to His purpose and plan.

Look at these simple truths expounded by Jeremiah and Isaiah. Jeremiah wrote: "'For I know the plans that I have for you,' declares the LORD, 'plans for welfare and not for calamity to give you a future and a hope'" (Jer. 29:11). God promises that Israel can seek and find Him and be gathered together in peace. God's purpose has always been for us to be at peace with God, ourselves, and others. Yet in our rebellion we have become alienated. The prophet Isaiah graphically describes our condition:

> But the wicked are like the tossing sea,
> For it cannot be quiet,
> And its waters toss up refuse and mud.
> "There is no peace," says my God,
> "for the wicked." (Isa. 57:20–21)

We will never know peace when we live in rebellion against God.

You may be wondering how we, with our human failings, can ever be at peace with a God who is holy. That's a good question and one that can only be answered when we understand the full significance of the name Jehovah Shalom. Do you remember how the angelic messengers heralded the coming of Christ? "Glory to God in the highest, And on earth peace among men with whom He is pleased" (Luke 2:14). In John 14:27, Jesus promises His followers that He would give them peace of a different quality than what the world offered. Jesus is the Prince of Peace promised by the prophet Isaiah (Isa. 9:6); therefore, He alone can give us peace; He alone can reconcile sinners to a holy God. He lived a life without sin, and therefore He alone is qualified to pay the transaction price to reconcile man to God (2 Cor. 5:21). If you want to experience Jehovah Shalom, you must turn from your sin and accept Jesus' payment for your sin by inviting Him to come into your life.

Perhaps you are certain that you have accepted Christ as your personal Savior, and yet you know that you are not experiencing wholeness in your relationship with God or others. You couldn't say truthfully that you know true peace. Are you living in obedience to God's Word? Could it be that you, like Israel in the period of the judges, are repeating the cycle of sin and disobedience, and thus have forfeited your peace? Have you, like the people of Israel, treated God as a nonentity, ignoring His Word and taking His blessings for granted? Have you craved for the riches of the land more than you crave for the approval of God? If so, you must return to the source of peace—Jehovah Shalom. Repent for areas of disobedience. Resolve to obey His statutes and ask God to create in you a pure heart. Involve yourself in His mission to make Himself known to the nations.

There is no peace for the wicked and there is no peace when we ignore God's purpose and His statutes. We are like the waters that cast up their dirt and mire. But the good news is that Jehovah Shalom wants to reveal Himself to you. Place yourself before Him as an offering and see if He does not show Himself faithful.

Southern Kingdom, was tottering
dred years after the ten northern
into captivity, Judah now stood in
e they, too, had been disobedient.
little from watching the spiritual
orthern Kingdom. It is a sad fact
vantage of the lessons that history

his time was a prophet named
uring the reign of Josiah, one of
ment history. Israel's history had
highs and lows, and frequently
al productivity of these periods
tual qualities of the king. Josiah
ings Manasseh and Amon, who
ritual and moral decline.

in the Books of Kings and
each king's reign, one of two
ign of that king. It simply says
in the sight of the Lord or that
t of the Lord. It is interesting
e ultimate question is whether
ht of the Lord. Ultimately, the
nation will be determined to
. I find it interesting that as a
r character matters when it
ild be a high priority, because
tion.

and Amon, were followed by
rofoundly moved when, as a
rd of God, which led him to

restore the temple and revive worship. These steps led to great
spiritual reforms. Unfortunately, the revival and reform ended
abruptly after the young king's untimely death. The wholesome
spiritual conditions in Judah quickly degenerated and the spiritual decline ultimately led to increased moral decay within the
nation. Oppression, violence, and political unrest were once
again the order of the day.

The condition in Judah had deteriorated to such an extent
that God declared the end of the kingdom of Judah: "However,
the LORD did not turn from the fierceness of His great wrath
with which His anger burned against Judah, because of all the
provocations with which Manasseh had provoked Him. And the
LORD said, 'I will remove Judah also from My sight, as I have
removed Israel. And I will cast off Jerusalem, this city I have chosen and the temple of which I said, "My name shall be there."' "
(2 Kings 23:26–27).

Can you imagine such a situation? The ten tribes of Israel
had already been taken into captivity. Several generations had
passed and the people of Judah had seen the evidence of moral
corruption and disobedience to God's Word. If they had seen the
fall of Israel, why could they not see the potential impact of their
own disobedience?

When I read the Old Testament accounts of the time of the
kings, I feel like I am reading today's headlines. Are we failing to
see the obvious moral decline in our nation and the resulting
corruption and lawlessness? Do we ignore the spiritual decline
and apathy in our own lives that frequently lead to disobedience? Often the symptoms are minor in the early stages of spiritual stagnation. Like the people of Judah, we first lose interest in
spiritual things; our Bible study and church attendance begin
slowly to atrophy. The spiritual decline creeps into our attitudes,

our work, our play, and our family time. If we do not rediscover God's Word in our lives and allow it to bring reform, we will find ourselves in a spiritual bondage that was worse than the captivity of the Old Testament.

GOD'S PROPHETIC SPOKESMAN

Into the midst of this spiritual decay, God sent a spokesman to proclaim the word of the Lord. Jeremiah and his message were not well received by the kings. To understand the significance of the wonderful name, *Jehovah Tsidkenu,* it is important that we look at the prophet's message in its historical setting.

Nebuchadnezzar, king of Babylon, had become a nemesis to Judah. King Zedekiah sent two priests to Jeremiah with the request that he inquire of the Lord on their behalf. "'Please inquire of the LORD on our behalf, for Nebuchadnezzar king of Babylon is warring against us; perhaps the LORD will deal with us according to all His wonderful acts, that the enemy may withdraw from us'" (Jer. 21:2). On the surface, this appears to be a reasonable request for a king to make of a prophet. Perhaps, like Zedekiah, you might have been expecting a favorable word from the prophet.

Listen to the prophet's response. "'Thus says the LORD God of Israel, "Behold, I am about to turn back the weapons of war which are in your hands, with which you are warring against the king of Babylon and the Chaldeans who are besieging you outside the wall; and I shall gather them into the center of this city. And I Myself shall war against you with an outstretched hand and a mighty arm, even in anger and wrath and great indignation"'" (21:4–5). Not exactly the good news scenario that Zedekiah was expecting when he sent the messenger to God's

— II —

JEHOVAH TSIDKEN

THE LORD IS O RIGHTEOUSNE

"In His days Judah will be saved,
And Israel will dwell securely;
And this is His name by which He will be
'The LORD our righteousness.'"

JEREMIAH 23:6

spokesman. Essentially, God tells Zedekiah that Babylon will be an instrument of His judgment. Not only will the Chaldeans storm the city; God will allow them into the center of the city. The attack will lead to a great pestilence, and those who happen to survive the pestilence, the sword, and the famine, God will hand over to Nebuchadnezzar (21:6–7).

Still, the Lord is compassionate and longsuffering, and He offers Judah the opportunity for repentance. In chapter 22, we discover that the Lord sends Jeremiah to the king of Judah with a word of compassion. "'Thus says the LORD, "Do justice and righteousness, and deliver the one who has been robbed from the power of his oppressor. Also do not mistreat or do violence to the stranger, the orphan, or the widow; and do not shed innocent blood in this place. For if you men will indeed perform this thing, then kings will enter the gates of this house, sitting in David's place on his throne, riding in chariots and on horses, even the king himself and his servants and his people"'" (Jer. 22: 3–4).

The Lord offers an opportunity to Zedekiah. If the king would bring forth the fruit of repentance, he would enter the gates of the house of the king and sit on David's throne. But if he failed to obey the prophet's words, Zedekiah was warned that his house would become a desolation. Zedekiah ignored the warning of the prophet and rejected the kindness of the Lord. He imprisoned Jeremiah in the court of the guard because Zedekiah didn't want to hear the prophet's words of judgment. Jeremiah told Zedekiah that he would see Nebuchadnezzar face to face, because he would be taken to Babylon as a captive (Jer. 32:1–5).

The people of Judah must have wondered how to understand Jeremiah's message in the light of God's promises and His

purpose for His people. Had God not promised to establish David's kingdom and his throne forever? Would captivity in Babylon not mean the defeat of God's own purpose? Into this environment of foreboding and gloom, the prophet held out a great word of hope. He promised that Israel would return from captivity and be restored to its homeland. You may recall that Jeremiah bought a relative's field in Anathoth. This was a dramatic action that graphically portrayed the hope for the future of God's people. The prophet had a word from the Lord that was even more dramatic and encouraging than this promise of a return from captivity. God would raise up from the line of David a righteous branch, a king who would reign and bring judgment and justice to the earth. He would be called Jehovah, our Righteousness—Jehovah Tsidkenu.

GOD'S PROMISE REVEALED IN HIS NAME

Jeremiah begins his message of encouragement with an indictment against the shepherds who have destroyed and scattered the flock of Israel. The Lord then promises that He will gather up his remnant and will raise up shepherds over them who will tend them and not be afraid any longer, nor will any of his people be missing (Jer. 23:1–4).

The incredible good news is the announcement that God will raise a righteous branch to reign as king:

> "Behold, the days are coming," declares the
> LORD,
> "When I shall raise up for David a righteous
> Branch;
> And He will reign as king and act wisely

> And do justice and righteousness in the land.
> In His days Judah will be saved,
> And Israel will dwell securely;
> And this is His name by which He will be called,
> The LORD our righteousness." (Jer. 23:5–6)

There is a striking similarity between the name *Tsidkenu* and *Zedekiah,* who was told by Jeremiah that he would be taken into captivity. The name *Zedekiah* means "the righteousness of Yahweh [Jehovah]." Originally, Zedekiah's name was *Mattaniah,* which means "a gift of Jehovah." Nebuchadnezzar placed Zedekiah on the throne in the place of his nephew Jehoiakin (2 Kings 24:17) and changed Mattaniah's name to Zedekiah. Scholars differ in their interpretation of the meaning of this name change. Some believe that the changing of the name was an intentional and scathing rebuke by Nebuchadnezzar of both the king and Israel's God. We often forget that what we do reflects upon our God. Could the changing of names have been a subtle reminder of what might have been for God's people and their king had they been obedient to God? It is more likely that the changing of names by the pagan king simply demonstrated the authority which Nebuchadnezzar had over the king of Judah. It is difficult for us to fully comprehend the devastating impact of the Babylonian captivity on the people of God. Yet the promise implicit in this name Jehovah Tsidkenu, so similar to the name of the captive king, tells us that God is still the sovereign and righteous ruler of the universe.

In the preceding chapters we learned that God revealed Himself as Jehovah Jireh, the Provider. Yet here we see His people in a captive situation lacking provision. He revealed His desire to be Jehovah Rophe to them, the Healer who would turn the bitter experiences of life to sweet; but here we see a people who are broken and in need of healing. As Jehovah Nissi, He promised to be their victorious Banner, but here they have been sorely and completely defeated. Refusing to sanctify themselves to Jehovah Mekadesh, they had become a corrupt and degenerate people. They had forsaken Jehovah Shalom and now they had lost their peace; they were torn by internal dissension and outward aggression. True to His character, God was always faithful to His promise, but Israel had turned their backs on Him and not their faces (Jer. 32:33).

Let me ask you about your own personal experience as you have studied these names and have pondered the nature of God. Do you know God's provision? Are you living in God's provision? If He is a God who heals, are you still struggling with bitter experiences of life? Are you living daily in spiritual victory? Since He is the source of peace, have you discovered a lack of anxiety and conflict in your life and relationships? For us, as for the Israelites, the name Jehovah Tsidkenu stands as a beacon of hope. Once more His children had been promised that they could be redeemed, healed, cleansed, victorious, and at peace through the Branch of Righteousness.

THE IMPLICATIONS OF JEHOVAH TSIDKENU

The name *Tsidkenu* comes from the root word *tsedek,* meaning "stiff" or "straight." It is difficult to translate the richness of this Hebrew word into English, but it has to do with God's dealing with His created beings. Let's look at several interrelated passages. In Leviticus 19:35–36, we find the demand that God's people employ just weights and measures. The reason behind this demand was singular. Their God is just and therefore His people must reflect His character in all of their dealings. In Deuteronomy 25:15–16, the use of just weights and measures is one of the conditions of abiding in the Promised Land. God required that His people appoint judges and officers who would judge the people with righteousness (Deut. 16:18). For God's people to act unjustly would be an abomination to the Lord. The whole spectrum of Israel's life was to be conducted in righteousness as a reflection of Jehovah Tsidkenu.

Have you thought about the implications for your personal life when you declare that you bear the name of Christ? Every aspect of your life must express the nature of the one who is Lord. Many non-Christians make their assessment of Christianity by the evidence they see in our lives. We must live in the light that our Lord is Jehovah Tsidkenu.

The truth behind the name Jehovah Tsidkenu speaks to another matter in our day. Our nation is becoming more pluralistic and syncretistic. As belief systems multiply, there is growing pressure to treat them all as though they are equally true and lead to the same god. This, in turn, has led to a dissolution of absolute values. Some would argue that truth is relative and that there are no absolute standards that define righteousness. This compromise has led to moral confusion, which, left unchecked, will lead to chaos.

Have you ever heard someone say, "I don't believe a certain action is right, but who am I to say what is right or wrong?" Perhaps you have made such a statement yourself or you have heard a Christian friend make such a statement in reference to moral issues such as abortion or homosexuality. We don't want to sound judgmental or appear narrow in our thinking, but we must ask ourselves if there are any moral absolutes, and if so, who determines them?

I suppose that most thinking persons would agree that our very survival demands that there be agreed-upon absolutes. For example, we wouldn't dream of taking our car on the road without some assurance that we could depend on other drivers to obey agreed-upon standards for staying in the proper lane, driving on the right side of the road, and obeying traffic signals. So we might ask how we establish agreed-upon moral standards for our nation. No human system will prove satisfactory. The only standard of righteousness is God. He is righteous and as Creator He established the world with moral standards which reflected His own nature.

A PERSONAL ENCOUNTER

Once, while witnessing on an airplane, I engaged my seatmate in a dialogue concerning several of the ultimate questions of life, such as: Who am I? How did I get here? How should I live? and Where am I going? As we discussed how a person should live, we began to talk about moral values. He agreed that values today seem topsy-turvy. Actions that were once considered immoral are viewed today as alternative lifestyles. Then he asked how anyone could determine what was right and wrong.

I asked him if I could attempt to answer the question, and he was more than willing to listen. I told him that there are only three options available to us in determining values. First, we could allow everyone to decide individually what is right and wrong. He immediately replied that such a solution would lead to chaos and was unworkable.

Another option would be to vote democratically on moral values and follow majority rule. He warmed to this suggestion, indicating that such a system would be fair and would explain why issues such as abortion were deemed wrong in the past but are now considered available options. I responded that while such a system seems fair, it is tragically flawed. I then illustrated:

"Suppose that a few minutes ago, while you were in the restroom, the captain told us that the plane was about 160 pounds overweight and that this weight differential was causing a problem. The passengers took a vote while you were away and the majority determined that you should be thrown out of the plane to resolve the problem." He immediately responded that he did not agree with our vote and insisted that the decision was unfair. I replied that the majority had deemed that it was a fair solution. In exasperation, he declared that our solution was immoral. At this point I agreed, but then I asked him why he had used words like *fair* and *moral*. Where had they originated?

He responded that he wasn't sure, but he knew that some things just weren't right, no matter how we might vote. I again agreed and told him that our sense of moral values is derived from the God who created the universe. His very character is such that He is fair and just. He is a righteous God and He created the universe to reflect His own nature. In fact, the only standard of righteousness is God.

I am grieved over a nation that promotes a phony peace. I am sick of the media promoting sexual promiscuity under the guise of alternative lifestyles. I am tired of a nation that glorifies needless violence and vilifies prayer and holiness. If we do not return to Jehovah Tsidkenu, the God of righteousness, I fear that we may be held captive to our own desires.

The Psalms consistently focus on the righteousness of God. In Psalm 85, the psalmist cries out for restoration and revival. Then he declares that God will speak peace to His godly ones (v. 8). Listen to this beautiful description of restoration:

Lovingkindness and truth have met together;
Righteousness and peace have kissed each other.
Truth springs from the earth;
And righteousness looks down from heaven.
Indeed, the LORD will give what is good;
And our land will yield its produce.
Righteousness will go before Him,
And will make His footsteps into a way. (vv. 10–13)

In Psalm 89, the psalmist declares the glory of the Lord who has created the heavens and the earth. He then declares that:

Righteousness and justice are the foundation
  of Thy throne;
Lovingkindness and truth go before Thee.
How blessed are the people who know the joyful
  sound!
O LORD, they walk in the light of Thy countenance.
In Thy name they rejoice all the day,
And by Thy righteousness they are exalted.
(vv. 14–16)

Psalm 129:4 simply declares that the Lord is righteous.

FULFILLED IN CHRIST

When we fully comprehend the significance of the name Jehovah Tsidkenu, one of the first questions that floods our mind is, "How can a sinful person stand in the presence of a righteous God?" It is an age-old question which must ultimately be resolved. The prophet Isaiah, when he was praying for his nation, found himself in the presence of a holy God and knew himself to be undone, a man of unclean lips (Isa. 6:5). Ultimately, he declares that even his righteous deeds are like a filthy garment (Isa. 64:6).

The great apostle Paul, the author of much of the New Testament, saw his own righteous accomplishments as rubbish. He argued that if anyone could put confidence in earthly accomplishments, he could. "Circumcised the eighth day, of the nation of Israel, of the tribe of Benjamin, a Hebrew of Hebrews; as to the Law, a Pharisee; as to zeal, a persecutor of the church; as to the righteousness which is in the Law, found blameless" (Phil. 3:5–6). Why would this religious and morally upright man count his own righteousness as mere rubbish? Listen to his own words: "That I may gain Christ, and may be found in Him, not having a righteousness of my own derived from the Law, but that which is through faith in Christ, the righteousness which comes from God on the basis of faith" (vv. 8b–9).

Why would prophet and apostle both look at their own righteousness as filthy garments or mere rubbish? Both knew that God is the only standard of righteousness. In the Sermon on the Mount, the Lord Jesus was comparing the righteous actions of the Jewish people with that of the Gentiles. His conclusion is profound: "Therefore you are to be perfect, as your heavenly Father is perfect" (Matt. 5:48). We often want to compare our righteousness with someone less righteous. "I'm better than most of the people in your church!" That may be true, but the standard of righteousness is not religious people, but a righteous God, who is perfect in His righteousness.

I know you must be thinking that the standard is impossible. You are right. And you have come to the same conclusion as the prophet and the apostle. You cannot earn God's favor; you cannot stand before a righteous God on your own merit. Still, there is good news. Jesus Christ is our Jehovah Tsidkenu. The fulfillment of Jeremiah's prophecy came in Jesus Christ. He is the Holy Branch raised up from the root of David. He is both the manifestation of perfect righteousness and the provision for our righteousness. He was fully man, yet without sin, and fully God so that He alone can represent sinful man before a holy God.

Look at 2 Corinthians 5:20–21: "Therefore, we are ambassadors for Christ, as though God were entreating through us; we beg you on behalf of Christ, be reconciled to God. He made Him who knew no sin to be sin on our behalf, that we might become the righteousness of God in Him." The only way sinful man can stand before Holy God is through faith in Jesus Christ. He is the Branch of David. Born of the virgin Mary, He was fully man and fully God. He fulfilled the promise of the Righteous One to come. He lived a sinless life, yet He died to pay the penalty of sin. To stand in righteousness before God, you must acknowledge your sin, be willing to turn from sin, and ask Christ to be your Jehovah Tsidkenu, your righteousness.

If you are not a Christian, stop now and pray. Simply ask Christ to come into your heart and forgive your sin. Tell a Christian friend about your decision and find a Bible-teaching church where you can publicly acknowledge your commitment to Christ.

If you already know Christ as Savior, you stand with His name, Jehovah Tsidkenu, emblazoned on you. It will impact the way you deal with your family. It will transform the way you do business and control your finances. Remember, God's righteousness demands just weights and measures. It requires that we practice justice and compassion in every arena of our lives.

12

JEHOVAH ROHI

THE LORD IS MY SHEPHERD

"The LORD is my shepherd;

I shall not want."

PSALM 23:1

If I were to ask you your favorite Bible verse, you might recite John 3:16. It was the first verse that many of us committed to memory, and it speaks of God's great love that brought us to salvation. If I were more specific and asked about your favorite psalm, you'd probably choose the Twenty-third Psalm.

The Spirit of God has used this psalm over the years to bring assurance and strength to many people who are struggling with difficult circumstances. As a pastor, I have frequently been asked to read Psalm 23 at the bedside of a sick patient or in the waiting room as someone's family member underwent surgery. Rarely have I officiated at a funeral where I have not included this great psalm. Military chaplains tell me that this writing has no rival among soldiers in tents and foxholes on the eve of a battle. When I was pastor at First Baptist in Norfolk, I sent a tape to our military personnel in Desert Storm which included a devotional based upon the Twenty-third Psalm.

In this chapter, we will discover a name for God which has become a favorite for many Christians. The name *Jehovah Rohi* means "the Lord my Shepherd." Some Bible scholars do not include Jehovah Rohi as a specific name like Jehovah Jireh, but because of its unique significance, I have chosen to include it here as worthy of our consideration.

The Setting for the Psalm

Probably written in the latter years of David's reign as Israel's king, this psalm is one of the most powerful and poignant passages to come from the pen of this prolific author. It clearly has the ring of personal experience. It speaks of a faith sobered by trials and a life mellowed and matured by the passing of years.

You will recall that David had experienced conflict, both internal and external, that included war, family dissolution, personal disappointments, discouragement, and despair that would equal or exceed the experiences of any of us today. David was a servant of God whose hands had been soiled by the murder of Uriah. His was a life marked by an adulterous relationship with Bathsheba and the ensuing family fighting that led to several deaths and ongoing conflict among his own family members. David experienced sin and sorrow; he knew the pain of the death of a young son and the rebellion of another son who tried to take his kingdom.

Yet this psalm tells us that, through it all, the king, who was a great warrior, had discovered God as His tender Shepherd. The imagery for this psalm takes us back to David's childhood when God had taken him from tending the sheep to anoint him as king. As a shepherd boy, David was deemed an unlikely candidate to become the king of Israel. I find it fascinating that the Spirit of God would bring David back to this simple but assuring picture of God as a gentle Shepherd caring for the need of His flock.

My father, a pastor for fifty-five years, was stricken with a malignant brain tumor in 1990. After surgery, the Lord gave him one more precious year of life. My dad often carried a couple of song sheets to church, requesting the minister of music to sing those particular songs. On the Sunday before my father died, my sister whispered in his ear, "It's Sunday, Daddy." He opened his eyes and quietly repeated a line from his hymn, "For all my sins, my Savior went to Calvary." These were the last intelligible words my dad uttered in this life. We like to think that he finished the hymn in the presence of his wonderful Shepherd. Like David, Dad had returned to the truths that were most basic in his life.

THE FUNDAMENTAL IDEA

The primary idea contained in the Hebrew term behind this name is "to feed" or "to lead to pasture." The term *rohi* often occurs in contexts that speak literally of shepherding, but our interest is in those passages where the figurative idea is implied. In Isaiah 44:28, God speaks of the Persian king Cyrus as functioning like a shepherd. Isaiah refers to Moses as a good shepherd (Isa. 63:11), who brought his people up out of the sea. In Jeremiah 3:15, the Lord promises that He will give His people good shepherds who will feed them with knowledge and understanding.

The prophets Isaiah and Jeremiah both depicted God as a shepherd. "Like a shepherd He will tend His flock, In His arm He will gather the lambs, And carry them in His bosom; He will gently lead the nursing ewes" (Isa. 40:11). "Hear the word of the LORD, O nations, and declare in the coastlands afar off, And say, 'He who scattered Israel will gather him, And keep him as a shepherd keeps his flock'" (Jer. 31:10).

One of the most important passages is found in Ezekiel 34, where God, as Shepherd, is contrasted with the false shepherds who have neglected His flock. God pronounces woe on the shepherds who have fed themselves and not the sheep. They have neglected the sickly and ignored those who have been scattered. The lack of attention of the shepherds has allowed the sheep to become prey for every beast of the field. Then the Lord declares that He Himself will perform the tasks of the shepherd:

> For thus says the Lord God, "Behold, I Myself will
> search for My sheep and seek them out. As a

shepherd cares for his herd in the day when he is among his scattered sheep, so I will care for My sheep and will deliver them from all the places to which they were scattered on a cloudy and gloomy day. And I will bring them out from the peoples and gather them from the countries and bring them to their own land; and I will feed them on the mountains of Israel, by the streams, and in all the inhabited places of the land. I will feed them in a good pasture, and their grazing ground will be on the mountain heights of Israel. There they will lie down in good grazing ground, and they will feed in rich pasture on the mountains of Israel. I will feed My flock and I will lead them to rest," declares the Lord GOD. "I will seek the lost, bring back the scattered, bind up the broken, and strengthen the sick; but the fat and the strong I will destroy. I will feed them with judgment." (vv. 11–16)

It is reassuring to know that God loves us, His sheep, so much that He Himself will care for us and deliver us on the gloomy days. Words such as *feed, care, gently lead, seek the lost, bind the broken, strengthen the sick* describe the tender nature of our God as He relates to His flock. He feeds us and nurtures us, bringing us to fertile grounds for grazing. It is His character as Shepherd that is seen in His care for His flock.

It is interesting that in 2 Samuel 5:2 we find a reference to David as a shepherd. The tribes are gathered to anoint him as king. In the process they declare: "Previously, when Saul was king over us, you were the one who led Israel out and in.

And the LORD said to you, 'You will shepherd My people Israel, and you will be a ruler over Israel.'" Notice both the term *shepherd* and the allusion to leading the sheep in and out. No doubt the idea that he as king was to shepherd God's people must have been in David's mind as he reflected on God's tender leadership in his life even during those gloomy days of sin and brokenness.

GOD AS OUR SHEPHERD

I would encourage you to read Psalm 23 before you continue reading the remainder of this chapter. Pay particular attention to the personal pronouns both as they relate to David and to God. You may want to underline them in your Bible as a constant reminder that this psalm is talking about a very personal relationship that you have with the God of the universe.

My Shepherd

The profound impact of Psalm 23 is not the discovery that God is our Shepherd, but the intimacy of the truth that He is *my* Shepherd. It is *my* Shepherd who makes *me* lie down in green pastures and leads *me* beside still waters. David knew that he belonged to the Lord, and it was that truth that gave him the greatest sense of strength.

I enjoy sitting in the shopping mall and watching the people who parade past. To say they are all different doesn't do justice to the variety that God has designed into the human race. We come in all sizes and shapes, colors and hues. We manifest different tastes in the way we dress, wear our hair, and decorate our bodies. We can identify persons by their fingerprints, their unique dental records, or their DNA. There are no two people alike. This not only shows God's creativity and His wonderful sense of humor; it also tells us that He loves each of us individually and distinctively. We often take it for granted that God made us as unique individuals. I suppose He could have cloned us. He could have created two prototypes, one Adam and one Eve, and then made all of us to look, think, respond, dress, and act alike. It would help with remembering names and no one would be concerned about their looks, but it would be *boring.*

The Creator of the universe fashioned each of us distinctively and uniquely to be who we are, but His individual concern did not cease at the point of creation. As the Good Shepherd, He knows His sheep by name. This singular thought is so profound that it defies our comprehension. The personal pronouns in the Twenty-third Psalm create a unique picture of a shepherd who lives with his flock, serves as their guide, caregiver, and protector. David could look back over his life and declare, "The Lord is *my* shepherd."

The nature of our God is a far cry from what we see in other world religions and the growing New Age religion. Most of the gods of other religions are either capricious and cruel, or vague and distant. Proponents of New Age look for the god in themselves or in an impersonal universe. Their only hope is that one day they will become one with the nothingness of the universe. Personally, I look forward to eternal life in the presence of a God who has revealed Himself to be our Shepherd. He is the God who formed me in my mother's womb, the one who has been my Provider and Protector throughout my life, and who has shepherded me through the dark valleys of life. Knowing I will spend eternity praising and serving Him brings me great joy.

I Shall Not Want

My good friend and mentor, Mark Corts, likes to refer to the early church in Jerusalem as a "no need" church. He takes this phrase from Acts 2:45 where Luke tells us that the early Christians were willing to sell property and share their resources to meet whatever need they might discover among those in the community. The early church was simply expressing the nature of their God, whose desire it is to provide for the needs of His sheep. David's simple expression of trust and provision is profound in its simplicity: "I shall not want." This phrase indicates that the shepherd is committed to meet the needs of the sheep.

In Psalm 23, the green pastures and quiet waters are mentioned first because they are priority needs of the sheep if they are to survive and grow. The green pastures and quiet waters speak both of rest and sustenance. The sheep cannot continue on the journey without sufficient rest and food. This picture also shows the intimate concern of the shepherd for the sheep. The shepherd may have to travel a long distance or put himself at risk to lead his sheep to that which meets their most basic needs.

As Christians, we often have trouble distinguishing between our "needs" and our "wants." Sometimes we want things that we truly don't need and that would be injurious to us if we were to receive them. The Shepherd knows His sheep so well that He knows their needs and provides for them. Notice, too, that the implications of the psalm are that sustenance is discovered only as the sheep follow the shepherd. He will lead them to quiet waters and green pastures, but if they fail to follow the Shepherd, they may well find themselves with unresolved needs.

Have you noticed that your satisfaction level is directly related to your proximity to the Good Shepherd?

If you continually find yourself with unrequited wants, ask yourself several questions. Is this a "want" or a "need?" Could it be that the Good Shepherd is protecting me from something that would be harmful? Is there something I need to learn or experience as I wait for the Shepherd's provision? If these questions don't yield any fruit, ask yourself, "Am I closely following my Shepherd?" Is there sin in my life that keeps me separated from the One who desires to lead me to still waters? Have I spent sufficient time resting in the green pastures of His care? We can become so rushed and harried that we experience want from sheer physical fatigue. Have I fed sufficiently from His Word as the food of life that provides the energy for my spiritual journey? When you follow the Shepherd closely, His will and desires will become your will and desires. You can trust the Good Shepherd to be consistent with His own nature.

He Restores My Soul

There are two possible ways for understanding the implications of the phrase "He restores my soul." "Restoration" may mean that a straying sheep has been brought back to the fold, thus experiencing full restoration. It is also possible that the phrase may point to a deep renewal available to all sheep, based on their intimate relationship to the shepherd who by nature is their total caregiver. The two ideas are intimately intertwined and therefore both ideas may be implied as the shepherd manifests his concern that all his sheep be constantly renewed and refreshed. God's desire is that His sheep experience abundant life.

Don't overlook the fact that the green pastures and the still waters are the essential provision by which the shepherd restores the sheep for their journey. It is important for us to remember that the journey is not complete when the sheep reach the green pastures and the still waters. The sheep are only being restored so that they might continue the journey, which may well lead them through dark valleys before the day is done. Rest is always a means to an end. The Shepherd renews the sheep so that they might follow Him as He leads them in the paths of righteousness.

We sometimes debate whether it is better to rest in the Lord or serve Him. We may take the story of Mary and Martha as a model and argue that we should place a priority on resting in Him. The truth is that the two ideas are corollary to one another, not opposite. We must learn to rest in the Lord and to find our refreshing in Him so that we might follow Him in service.

He Guides Me in the Paths of Righteousness

"He guides me in the paths of righteousness" simply means that when we follow the Shepherd we will always be on the right paths. They will be safe and productive because of His presence. Being on the right path does not mean that we will not face danger or difficulty as we follow the Shepherd. In verse 4, the reader is reminded that the sheep may have to travel through the valley of death, yet the sheep are assured that no evil will befall them if they remain near the shepherd. We frequently desire and plead that we might avoid the difficult circumstances of life, when in truth our greatest concern should always be our proximity to the Shepherd.

The apostle Paul could rejoice and worship in prison because he was assured of the Good Shepherd's presence. You may be wondering how anyone can be certain that following Christ will assure that they are in the right path. The answer is found in the refrain, "For His name's sake." As we have already noted, the name of God points to His character. In other words, God always acts in harmony with His own character. The Good Shepherd would never lead His sheep in paths that would prove harmful or destructive. You can trust the Creator to be your Good Shepherd.

I Fear No Evil

In the first section of the psalm, the shepherd is pictured as a guide who scouts the landscape to find the best place to lead his flock for food, water, and rest. Now he is seen as coming alongside to personally escort the flock. When the flock faces the testing of the dark valley and the specter of evil, he is by their side.

As we study the second section of this psalm, you will notice that the predominate pronoun is *I*. It appears that David becomes intentionally more personal as he declares, "I fear no evil; for Thou art with me. . . ." The shepherd is no longer pictured as being out in front leading the flock.

You may be familiar with the popular poem, *Footprints in the Sand*. For an extended period as we walk with the Lord, two sets of footprints are evident on the beach headed in the same direction. At a certain point, though, one set of footprints disappears. We are tempted to believe that we were abandoned by the Lord at that point in time, but we come to discover that the absence of one set of footprints means only that we were being carried by our Companion.

Most Christians have experienced dark valleys of fear, doubt, disappointment, and even death. It may be when we hear the diagnosis that we have, or a family member has, cancer. Dark valleys can come when we fail a test, lose a job, suffer a broken relationship, or experience the death of a loved one. When we are God's sheep, we can be assured that He is with us and that He is capable of defending us.

The rod and staff are the tools with which the shepherd can protect his sheep. The rod was a cudgel, worn at the belt, providing protection against animals and thieves. The staff provides protection for the sheep as the shepherd uses it to keep the sheep from straying off the path as they follow him. The staff of guidance may seem like a strict form of discipline until we observe that the shepherd's singular desire is to protect his sheep. When you experience the Shepherd prodding you back into line, do you ever react to that gentle disciplinary nudge with anger? You can trust the Shepherd to be concerned only for your care and protection. We often forget that God's discipline is always prompted by His unchanging love and is always consistent with His character. He must lead us back onto the right paths so that we will know His presence and experience His protection.

I Will Dwell in the House of the Lord Forever

As we conclude the beautiful shepherd psalm, the imagery of the sheep and shepherd is exchanged for an even more intimate picture. David now pictures himself as a guest in the Lord's house. In the world of the Old Testament, to be invited to someone's table created a bond of mutual loyalty and friendship. The host in Psalm 23 doesn't simply invite the guest to share his table and his home; he makes him an honored guest. He anoints his head with oil and provides for his every need with great abundance. The recipient declares, "My cup overflows."

To be invited to God's banquet table assures us that goodness and lovingkindness will be fully experienced throughout our lives. "Lovingkindness" refers to God's covenant love promised to His own people. Throughout the Bible, the people of God continually return to the bedrock truth that God is faithful and exhibits His goodness and lovingkindness to His people. Notice, too, David's conviction that he would dwell in the house of the Lord forever. God's relationship with His people is eternal in nature.

No matter what circumstances you face in your daily life, you can be assured that God is faithful and that He always responds according to His own nature. For that reason we know that he is not the author of evil, but works to redeem the evil. He works in every circumstance for our own good (Rom. 8:28). There may be those "dark valley" times when we cannot see the good, but we can always be assured that His lovingkindness will follow us all the days of our lives, and when life is over, we can look forward to His eternal presence.

JESUS, OUR GOOD SHEPHERD

Our study of the name Jehovah Rohi would be incomplete if we did not turn our attention to the pages of the New Testament. In John 10, Jesus tells His disciples a parable about a good shepherd. He contrasts the good shepherd with the stranger, the thief, the robber, and the hireling. The thief and the robber desire only to take advantage of the sheep. The hireling flees when there is a threat to the sheep. They are not his sheep and therefore he has no depth of commitment to their safety. In contrast, the Good Shepherd is willing to lay down His life for the sheep. Listen to these words, " 'I am the good shepherd; the good shepherd lays down His life for the sheep' " (10:11). For emphasis, Jesus repeats His profound declaration: "I am the good shepherd; and I know My own, and My own know Me, even as the Father knows Me and I know the Father; and I lay down My life for the sheep" (10:14–15).

Jesus, God in the flesh, fully revealed what it means to address God as Jehovah Rohi. He is the Lord, my Shepherd. He alone exhibited the shepherd's willingness and ability to lay down His life to save the sheep. Twice, in John 10:7 and 10:9 He declares Himself to be the door of the sheep. The shepherd would lay his own body across the entrance to the sheepfold, thus becoming the very point of access and protection for the sheep. Have you gained entrance to the sheepfold through Jesus Christ? You must first acknowledge your sin and need and then invite Jesus to become your personal Savior and Shepherd. Just tell Him of your need and your desire. Find a Christian friend or a pastor and tell him about the decision you have made.

If you know that Jesus is your Savior and Shepherd, then this passage contains an important reminder for you. Notice how the sheep are described in verses 3–4: "'And the sheep hear his voice, and he calls his own sheep by name, and leads them out. When he puts forth all his own, he goes before them, and the sheep follow him because they know his voice.'" Two of the characteristics of genuine sheep are that they know the Shepherd's voice and they follow Him. The sheep benefit from the presence of the Shepherd; therefore, when they hear His voice, they seek to follow Him. *As we learn to live in the presence of the Lord, we discover the intimacy of His shepherding nature.*

Have you spent sufficient time in prayer and Bible study to know the voice of the Shepherd? Have you come to understand His character so well that you trust Him in every circumstance of life? When you are weary or wounded, do you trust Him to gently lead you? Do you believe that He desires to anoint your head and heal your wounds? At the end of a difficult day or week, do you know that it is His nature to bring you safely into His fold? Are you living daily by these simple truths? The intimate knowledge of Jesus your Shepherd will enable you to rejoice always (1 Thess. 5:16), to give thanks in every circumstance, (1 Thess. 5:18), and to live an anxiety-free life (Phil. 4:6).

We should look at one final picture before we conclude our study of Jehovah Rohi:

> For this reason, they are before the throne of God; and they serve Him day and night in His temple; and He who sits on the throne shall spread His tabernacle over them. They shall hunger no more, neither thirst anymore; neither shall the sun beat down on them, nor any heat; for the Lamb in the center of the throne shall be their shepherd, and shall guide them to springs of the water of life; and God shall wipe every tear from their eyes.
> (Rev. 7:15–17)

The beautiful image and reality of a loving Shepherd is a truth for this life and the life to come. Although the text from Revelation 7 is specifically referring to those who have come through the great tribulation, the truth can be applied to every believer. When we "dwell in His house forever," we are assured that the Lamb of God, slain before the foundation of the world, will lead us to the springs of water of life and wipe away every tear from our eyes. What a marvelous and mysterious truth we have discovered. The Good Shepherd is the Lamb of God who lays down His life for the sheep, and the Lamb of God is the Good Shepherd.

13

JEHOVAH SHAMMAH

THE LORD IS THERE

"And the name of the city from that day shall be,

'The LORD is there.'"

EZEKIEL 48:35B

The last name of God in the Old Testament is found in the final verse of the Book of Ezekiel. It is the name *Jehovah Shammah,* which is translated, "Jehovah is there." As we explore the historical setting for this passage, we will note that it is a most fitting name with which Old Testament revelation comes to a climax.

The name Jehovah Shammah contains both promise and a sense of fulfillment. It focuses on God's personal presence as it relates to His purpose in the redemption of mankind.

THE PROPHET'S WORLD

The prophet Ezekiel declared the word of the Lord at a time when the nation of Israel was totally decimated. The people of Israel were physically, emotionally, and spiritually bankrupt because of the Babylonian captivity. As you read the Book of Ezekiel, try to put yourself in the place of an Israelite from that era. Jerusalem has been sacked and the temple, the place standing for God's visible presence, has been destroyed. The prophetic utterance that contains the name Jehovah Shammah can be dated about fourteen years after the destruction of the temple.

The days leading up to the Babylonian captivity were marked by sin and rebellion. The prophet described Israel as a ruined vine (Ezek. 19). In chapter 20, he rehearses God's dealings with Israel and declares that God must pour out His wrath upon this nation that has defiled itself. Throughout this section you will find the declaration that God has acted for the sake of His name (Ezek. 20:9, 44). God is a holy God and therefore He cannot permit unholiness among His people to continue unabated. He must respond according to His own nature.

The prophet Ezekiel groans with a broken heart as he is required to deliver this message of judgment. "'As for you, son of man, groan with breaking heart and bitter grief, groan in their sight. And it will come about when they say to you, "Why do you groan?" that you will say, "Because of the news that is coming; and every heart will melt, all hands will be feeble, every spirit will faint, and all knees will be weak as water. Behold, it comes and it will happen," declares the Lord GOD'" (Ezek. 21:6–7). In chapter 22, the prophet declares their many transgressions against the holiness of God. They have treated father and mother without regard, despised holy things and profaned the sabbath, practiced sexual promiscuity, taken bribes, and oppressed the weak. Their political and religious leaders have not rebuked the people in their sin, but they have led in the rebellion. The Lord declares that He had searched for a man who would build a wall and stand in the gap before Him for the land. Not one was found (22:30). For their rebellion, the Lord declares that He must bring judgment upon His people (24:14).

In chapter 33, we begin to see the turning point. Ezekiel is appointed as God's watchman. God instructs the watchman to tell His people that He takes no pleasure in the death of the wicked, but desires that they turn back from their evil ways and live (33:11). Thus the prophet is to declare the message of repentance accompanied by holiness. Rather than blaming the Lord for the calamity that has befallen them, they are to turn from their own unrighteousness and practice justice and righteousness (33:17–20).

Next, Ezekiel is instructed to pronounce judgement upon the false shepherds who have neglected God's flock. In this context we begin to hear the promise of restoration:

"And I will bring them out from the peoples
and gather them from the countries and bring
them to their own land; and I will feed them on the
mountains of Israel, by the streams, and in all the
inhabited places of the land. I will feed them in a
good pasture, and their grazing ground will be on
the mountain heights of Israel. There they will lie
down in good grazing ground, and they will feed
in rich pasture on the mountains of Israel. I will
feed My flock and I will lead them to rest," declares
the Lord GOD. (34:13–15)

Through the prophet Ezekiel, God reveals that His good
shepherd will be His servant David. " 'Then I will set over them
one shepherd, My servant David, and he will feed them; he will
feed them himself and be their shepherd. And I, the LORD, will
be their God, and My servant David will be prince among them;
I, the LORD, have spoken' " (Ezek. 34:23–24). Does this remind
you of our study of Jehovah Rohi in the last chapter? We are
again reminded of the coming Messiah, one who in His incarnation is fully God, Jesus.

Ezekiel prophesies that the mountains of Israel will be blessed.
" 'But you, O mountains of Israel, you will put forth your branches
and bear your fruit for My people Israel; for they will soon come.
For, behold, I am for you, and I will turn to you, and you shall be
cultivated and sown. And I will multiply men on you, all the house
of Israel, all of it; and the cities will be inhabited, and the waste
places will be rebuilt' " (36:8–10).

Why is God bringing about this restoration? Remember
that God had to bring judgment because Israel had profaned His
name. God is now prepared to restore a repentant people

because it is consistent with His nature to do so, thus it is for His name's sake:

> "Therefore, say to the house of Israel, 'Thus says the Lord God, "It is not for your sake, O house of Israel, that I am about to act, but for My holy name, which you have profaned among the nations where you went. And I will vindicate the holiness of My great name which has been profaned among the nations, which you have profaned in their midst. Then the nations will know that I am the LORD" declares the Lord GOD, "when I prove Myself holy among you in their sight."'" (36:22–23)

This wonderful declaration is followed by the promise that He will gather them, cleanse them, give them a new heart, put His Spirit within them and cause them to observe His ordinances (vv. 24–27). In response to God's direction, Ezekiel prophesies to the valley of dry bones and commands them to live (ch. 37).

In chapters 40–48, we read about God's wonderful plans for the restoration of His people. Many of these plans are focused on the rebuilding of the temple. Don't forget the central place the temple plays in Israel's life as it symbolizes God's presence among them. In a vision, Ezekiel is given the measurement for the outer and inner courts, as well as other details about the construction of the temple (chs. 40–42). The focus and purpose of the restoration and the rebuilding of the temple is most clearly articulated in 43:4–5: "And the glory of the LORD came into the house by the way of the gate facing toward the east. And the Spirit lifted me up and brought me into the inner court; and behold, the glory of the LORD filled the house." The glory of the Lord refers to His presence. He will be present among His people.

The remainder of this final section talks about the Levites' duties, the ordinances for the priest, and the various offerings to be brought before the Lord, as well as the division of the land. Look now at chapter 48 of Ezekiel. The tribes and their dwelling places are spelled out at great length, but don't let all the detail distract you from the wonderful promise contained in the very last verse. " 'The city shall be 18,000 cubits round about; and the name of the city from that day shall be, "The Lord is there." ' "

The message of hope and restoration must have been a ray of hope to a people in captivity. The prophet looks forward to the day when Israel will be resettled by God's people and the temple rebuilt. But the issue is not simply a physical building, it is the glory and presence of the Lord. Jehovah Shammah means "the Lord is there." Israel will once again know His presence. Let's take a short overview of Israel's history to see the significance contained in the promise of this name.

ISRAEL'S UNIQUE RELIGION

At this point, it might be helpful to remember one of the unique aspects of Israel's religion. When you contrast Judaism with the religions of the surrounding nations, you will note Israel's distinctive conviction that Holy God dwelled in their midst. He was not an absentee landlord represented by some carved idol or a limited deity relegated to a particular holy place. He was a personal and all-powerful God present with them at all times and in all places.

You may recall that when we discussed the name Yahweh [Jehovah], we noticed the promise of God's assurance that He would be with Moses when he visited Pharaoh and led the people of Israel from captivity. When Moses decried his own inability, God responded: "Certainly I will be with you" (Exod. 3:12).

Moses lived his entire life with this bedrock promise in mind. Let me give you one example. After the giving of the Ten Commandments, Moses returned from Mt. Sinai to find that Israel had committed a great sin by constructing a golden calf to be their god. "Now when the people saw that Moses delayed to come down from the mountain, the people assembled about Aaron, and said to him, 'Come, make us a god who will go before us; as for this Moses, the man who brought us up from the land of Egypt, we do not know what has become of him'" (Exod. 32:1). The Lord tells Moses that he will send an angel before him, but that He cannot go up in their midst because of their obstinate sin (Exod. 33:3). Moses responds that if he has found favor in God's sight he must know God's ways. Listen now to the dialogue:

> "Now therefore, I pray Thee, if I have found favor in Thy sight, let me know Thy ways, that I may know Thee, so that I may find favor in Thy sight. Consider too, that this nation is Thy people," And He said, "My presence shall go with you, and I will give you rest" Then he said to Him, "If Thy presence does not go with us, do not lead us up from here. For how then can it be known that I have found favor in Thy sight, I and Thy people? Is it not by Thy going with us, so that we, I and Thy

people, may be distinguished from all the other
people who are upon the face of the earth?"

(Exod. 33:13–16)

The distinctive characteristic of the people of God is that
He is personally present with them.

The pillar of fire, the cloud, the movable tabernacle, and finally
the permanent temple were all symbolic of the presence of God
with His people. When the cloud stood over the tabernacle, the
people were assured of God's presence and they stopped to worship.
The cloud that surrounded the mountain when God gave Moses
the Ten Commandments made the people aware that they were in
the presence of a holy God.

The passion that filled David's heart to build a permanent
temple was related to his desire to have a permanent place to
signify God's presence. God, through Nathan the prophet, told
David that He does not dwell in a house. He assured David that
He had been with him wherever he had gone (1 Chron.
17:1–8). God did, however, promise that He would give His
people a permanent place and allow David's descendants to
build a temple. When Solomon, David's son, completed the temple, it was filled with a thick cloud. The cloud symbolized the
glory, or presence of the Lord (2 Chron. 7:1–3).

At the time of Ezekiel's prophecy, the temple lay in ruins.
Israel was despondent and discouraged. It may have seemed to
many that God had removed His presence. Into this hopeless situation the prophecy of Ezekiel must have seemed like a ray of
light and hope. He declares that there will be a new temple built
and the name will be Jehovah Shammah, "the LORD is there."

The name Jehovah Shammah is a reminder in our darkest
hour that God is with us. When you are feeling abandoned and

hopeless, address Him as Jehovah Shammah. Read Psalm 139:1–12 and rejoice in His presence.

His Presence—The Incarnation

What does the new covenant reveal concerning the fulfillment of the promise implicit in the name Jehovah Shammah? We begin the New Testament with the wonderful story of the birth of Christ. Joseph, from the line of David, is told that his betrothed wife, Mary, would bear a son who had been conceived in her by the Holy Spirit. His name was to be called Jesus for He would save His people from their sin. The birth of Jesus would fulfill the prophecy of Isaiah. "'BEHOLD, THE VIRGIN SHALL BE WITH CHILD, AND SHALL BEAR A SON, AND THEY SHALL CALL HIS NAME IMMANUEL,' which translated means, 'GOD WITH US'" (Matt. 1:23).

Incredible, isn't it? Near the end of the period we call Old Testament times there was a prophecy promising God's abiding presence. At the beginning of the New Testament period we have the wonderful promise that in Jesus, we can know God's abiding presence. Jesus reveals and fulfills Jehovah Shammah.

In the Book of Colossians, Paul was dealing with a growing heresy that is similar in nature to the New Age emphasis of our day. People were interested in knowing the force behind the universe. One of the popular terms used in their speculation was the Greek word *pleroma,* which is translated *fulness.* Paul grasps this popular term and fills it with new meaning. After declaring that Jesus was the Redeemer, the image of the invisible God, the author of creation, and the head of the church, he makes an astounding declaration. "For it was the Father's good pleasure for all the fulness to dwell in Him" (Col. 1:19). The word *fulness* is the translation of the word *pleroma.* In

Jesus Christ, man came to know and experience the full presence of Holy God.

John, in his Gospel, echoes this same truth with terminology that causes us to think back to the Old Testament appearances of God. "And the Word became flesh, and dwelt among us, and we beheld His glory, glory as of the only begotten from the Father, full of grace and truth" (John 1:14). In Ezekiel, we saw God's glory as it filled the temple like a thick cloud. The glory of God refers to His revelation of Himself to us; it signifies His presence and His holiness. John declares that God's glory dwelt or tabernacled among us in the person of Jesus. We can see and know the presence of God as Jesus demonstrated God's grace and His truth. God's grace speaks of His lovingkindesss; His truth speaks to His holiness.

We see these qualities come together as the scribes and Pharisees bring to Jesus a woman caught in the act of adultery. They cite the law's requirement that she be stoned and then ask what Jesus would say. Jesus stoops and draws in the sand, asking whoever was without sin to cast the first stone. When the hostile crowd dissipates, He asks the woman about the absence of accusers and then declares: "Neither do I condemn you; go your way. From now on and sin no more" (John 8:11). By offering forgiveness, Jesus manifested God's grace; by demanding that she sin no more, He embodied God's truth.

The simple point is that Jesus embodied the presence of God. When we see Jesus we see the Father, for He and the Father are one. Jesus is Jehovah Shammah. God's presence was not to be known in a building or in a specific location, but in His Son, the abiding presence of Holy God is experienced in relationship with Jesus Christ.

GOD'S PRESENCE IN US

Some people follow the progress of the revelation of God's presence this far, but fail to make the next logical step. If God's presence was seen in the spectacular revelations of the Old Testament such as the burning bush and the pillar of fire, and then His presence was manifest in Jesus, where would one find the manifestation of His presence today? The clear answer of Scripture is that God wants to manifest His presence in the world through His people.

If we look further at John's Gospel, we find a section where Jesus is preparing His disciples for His departure. He tells them not to despair, that His departure will actually work for their advantage, because He will send the Holy Spirit to indwell them. The Spirit will convict the world of sin, righteousness, and judgment. He will guide the disciples into all truth and enable them to pray in Jesus' name (John 16). John 17 is often referred to as the high priestly prayer. Jesus first prays that He might glorify the Father in death as He did in His life (John 17:1–6). Jesus' prayer then focuses on His disciples and all those who would believe through their witness in the centuries to come (17:20). He prays that His followers would be guarded by the Father while they are in the world (17:10–11). He prays that they would have a full measure of His joy, that they would be sanctified in truth, and they would be one as He and the Father are one (17:13–21).

What is the bottom line of this prayer? Verse 18 gives us the first clue. "'As Thou didst send Me into the world, I also have sent them into the world.'" Why did God send Jesus into the world? He sent Him to manifest His glory, His presence. In case you think I have overly pressed the point, listen to verse 22: "'And the glory which Thou hast given Me I have given to them; that they may be one, just as We are one.'" God's glory, His powerful presence, is now to be manifest in us, His followers.

If you look back at the passage we referred to in Colossians 1 where Paul declared that Jesus was the full expression of God, you will discover that in that same context he talks about the church as Christ's body. This church is prepared by God to reveal a mystery which has been hidden from the ages past but is now manifested to His saints, "to whom God willed to make known what is the riches of the glory of this mystery among the Gentiles, which is Christ in you, the hope of glory" (Col. 1:27). The indwelling presence of Christ manifest in us through the Holy Spirit is what enables us to reveal God's presence today.

What a marvelous truth! God wants to indwell His people in such a way that Jehovah Shammah would be seen in us. This is the thrust of Paul's declaration in 1 Corinthians 3:16: "Do you not know that you are a temple of God, and that the Spirit of God dwells in you?" In that same context, Paul deals with the Corinthians' use of their gifts in service to the Lord. He tells them that there will be a judgment for the quality of our service which is built upon the foundation of Jesus Christ. In chapter 6, verse 19, he reminds them once again that their own bodies are temples of the Holy Spirit. In this instance he is forced to bring rebuke for the sin of immorality. He reminds them, "For you have been bought with a price: therefore glorify God in your body" (1 Cor. 6:20).

Statistics tell us that the incidence of divorce and sexual sin in the church is similar to that in the public at large. We are often reminded that 20 percent of the people in the average local church do 80 percent of the ministry. Too much is at stake to allow this imbalance to go unabated. Our holiness and our service are not simply a matter of do's and don'ts that seem strikingly out of date in present-day society. What is at stake is the purity and ministry of a people in whom the presence of God is to be manifested to a hurting and needy world.

If we desire that the Spirit of God would move upon our nation, we must set a higher standard of holiness and service among the people of God who are destined to manifest God's presence. *We are His temple and He is present in us.* This truth should impact how we spend our time, money, and energy. It must have an impact on the way we do business in the marketplace, how we treat our families, and how we engage our neighbors. If the world is to see the presence of Holy God, it will be in us.

The Ultimate Fulfillment of Jehovah Shammah

There is yet a final chapter to the fulfillment of the promise implicit in the name Jehovah Shammah. Jesus Himself promised His disciples that there would be a final stage of fulfillment related to God's presence. In John 14, as He was preparing His disciples for His departure, He declared that in His Father's house there were many dwelling places. His leaving enabled Him to prepare a place for His followers, so that, "where I am, there you may be also" (John 14:3). At the end of the high priestly prayer, we discover another wonderful truth about God's glory. Listen to Jesus' last request: "Father, I desire that they also, whom Thou hast given Me, be with Me where I am, in order that they may behold My glory, which Thou hast given Me; for Thou didst love Me before the foundation of the world" (17:24). We will be in His presence and behold His glory.

The psalmist looked forward to an ideal city where God's presence will be known:

> There is a river whose streams make glad the city
>   of God,
> The holy dwelling places of the Most High.
> God is in the midst of her, she will not be moved.
>
> (Ps. 46:4–5a)

The writer to the Hebrews tells us that Abraham was looking for the city whose architect and builder is God (11:10). Later, in chapter 12, the writer contrasts the new Mount Zion to the blazing fire on the mountain at the giving of the Ten Commandments. He then declares: "But you have come to Mount Zion and to the city of the living God, the heavenly Jerusalem, and to myriads of angels, to the general assembly and church of the first-born who are enrolled in heaven, and to God, the Judge of all, and to the spirits of righteous men made perfect, and to Jesus, the mediator of a new covenant, and to the sprinkled blood, which speaks better than the blood of Abel" (vv. 22–24).

Remember the story I told you in chapter 7 about the deacon who was dying of cancer? He had asked a group of his friends to meet with him for prayer. It was a high and holy time for all of us as we gathered around his bed, anointed his head with oil, and prayed. At the end of our time of prayer, he said, "Men, I'll never forget this day. We are still praying that God will work a miracle of healing." Then he raised his hand toward the heavens and declared, "But if He chooses not to heal me, I can hardly wait to see my Jesus." His words were much like the sentiment of the apostle Paul when he declared that he was hard pressed on each side. He wanted to remain and complete his work and yet there would be infinite joy when he stood in the presence of Holy God.

Ezekiel's prophecy will be ultimately fulfilled when death is swallowed up in victory and the new Jerusalem is inhabited by God's redeemed. No one describes the scene quite like John in the Book of Revelation: "And I saw a new heaven and a new earth; for the first heaven and the first earth passed away, and there is no longer any sea. And I saw the holy city, new Jerusalem, coming down out of heaven from God, made ready as a bride adorned for her husband. And I heard a loud voice from the throne, saying, 'Behold, the tabernacle of God is among men, and He shall dwell among them, and they shall be His people, and God Himself shall be among them'" (Rev. 21:1–3). "And he carried me away in the Spirit to a great and high mountain, and showed me the holy city, Jerusalem, coming down out of heaven from God, having the glory of God" (vv. 10–11a). "And I saw no temple in it, for the Lord God, the Almighty, and the Lamb, are its temple. And the city has no need of the sun or of the moon to shine upon it, for the glory of God has illumined it, and its lamp is the Lamb" (vv. 22–23).

Ezekiel's temple, which shall be called Jehovah Shammah, was not a temple constructed by human hands, but the temple of the New Jerusalem which is the Lord God Almighty and the Lamb.

TWO FINAL QUESTIONS

Do you know for certain that if you were to step out of this life and into the next, you would be in the presence of God? If you do not know Christ as your personal Savior, then your name is not written in the Lamb's Book of Life. This is not an issue of denominational pedigree or religious activity; this is a matter of the forgiveness of your sins through the only One qualified to do so, Jesus Christ, who is Jehovah Shammah.

If you are a Christian, then I must ask you, does your lifestyle demonstrate that God is present in you? Is His presence reflected in the way you do business? Do your language and lifestyle demonstrate the presence of God in your life? Do your personal relationships speak of His presence? If you answer no to any of these questions, it is time for you to turn from activities that do not speak of His presence and turn to Him. You are His temple; He desires to reveal Himself through you.

14

THE GROWING
RELATIONSHIP

*"Hear, O Israel! The LORD is our God, the LORD
is one! And you shall love the LORD your God
with all your heart and with all your soul
and with all your might."*

DEUTERONOMY 6:4–5

The Book of Deuteronomy picks up the story of Israel as they are poised to enter the Promised Land after an aborted attempt that had occurred nearly forty years earlier. The title of the book comes from a Greek word which means "second law." This does not indicate that Deuteronomy contains a new law, but rather that it is a restatement of the law to this new generation poised to enter the Promised Land. Thus the book repeats much of the material found in Exodus, Leviticus, and Numbers. The repetition was necessary to prepare this new generation of Israelites to enter and possess the Promised Land.

The people of Israel were about to enter a land where the people were polytheistic; they worshipped many gods. In light of this environment and challenge, it is not inappropriate or insignificant that Deuteronomy begins with a declaration of Israel's commitment to one God: The Lord is One. He alone is Holy God and beside Him all other gods are but pretenders. If you would take a moment and read Deuteronomy 6, you will find that the people of Israel are commanded to teach this truth about God to their children at every available moment. They are told to bind these words on their doorposts and gates. Literally, they were to saturate all of life's activities with the name and nature of God. Moses is concerned that when they have taken the land and have satisfied themselves with the plenty that God has provided, they will forget the Lord who brought them out of bondage and go after other gods.

When I read this warning, I cannot help but think about the application to our own situation. Do we cry out to God in our need and then forget Him in our prosperity? Do we seek Him in prayer and dedication when we find ourselves confronted by the difficult challenges of life and then look to our own self-sufficiency when things seem more settled? Are we tempted to turn to the gods of materialism and success and ignore the provision of the Lord?

As we read the further revelation of God contained in Scripture, we find that the one God revealed Himself in three persons: God the Father, God the Son, and God the Holy Spirit. For example, in Ephesians 1, Paul refers to all three persons of the Godhead at work in redemption. In verse 3, he blesses God as the God and Father of the Lord Jesus Christ. Paul talks about our redemption and forgiveness being found in Christ Jesus by the will of God. He declares that we were sealed in Him (Christ), by the Holy Spirit of promise.

This powerful passage from Deuteronomy stands as a backdrop against which we can review the names of God that have been a part of our study. This passage reminds us that God is One. The various names that we have discovered in our study of God's Word allow us to more fully comprehend the nature and character of God. It is as if we are turning a diamond in our hands and gazing as the light of revelation strikes a new and previously unexplored facet of the stone. God's names are a continual unveiling of His character in response to the unique challenges that Israel faced. These names enabled God's people to understand more fully the majesty and richness of His multifaceted character.

The names of God reflect God's desire to reveal Himself fully to mankind so that we might come to know Him and experience His fullness. The same is true today. God wants to reveal Himself fully to you that you might know and trust Him in every arena of your life. It is my prayer that this has become more than a Bible study for you, but has become a lifelong journey to know God in every area of your life.

THREE FOUNDATIONAL PRINCIPLES

We began our study with three foundational principles. First, the names were given by God, not developed by man. Some liberal scholars have attempted to analyze and divide the first books of the Bible by the various names used for God. Their assumption was that various writers and editors had written different parts of these books and had used different names in their attempt to explain God. I contend that the names are a distinctive part of God's self-revelation of His own nature. Each was revealed at a unique juncture in the journey of faith to allow His people to know of His desire and ability to supply their every need.

Second, the giving of the names demonstrates God's desire that we can fully know and worship Him. When we tell someone our name, we reveal a certain willingness to be known. The Bible records the wonderful story of God seeking to make Himself known to His creation. He is not simply a God who is there, but He is a God who speaks. God's desire is that you will come to know Him in a personal way.

Third, God's name, in each case, reveals a portion of His multi-faceted goodness and glory. God is so wonderful that our mind cannot comprehend nor can our tongue describe His glory, yet He daily makes Himself known so that we can grow in our understanding.

Elohim

You may have noticed that we began our study with the name Elohim, which was found in Genesis 1:1, and we concluded our study in Revelation 21, where we found the fulfillment of Jehovah Shammah, the God who is there. Elohim is generally translated as "God." It is derived either from the singular El, meaning "Lord," or from Eloah, which means "powerful one." Elohim is a plural form which has an intensifying effect, underlining the majesty of God's power. The context of Genesis 1:1 makes it abundantly clear that the powerful God of the universe created all that exists.

The singular statement, "In the beginning God created the heavens and the earth," should fill you with mystery and awe. This statement stands in direct contrast to an atheistic evolutionary model of how everything came into being. The significance of God as Creator means that you exist not by accident of some chance evolutionary process but by the direct creative purpose of God who is the Author of everything. As we read further in Genesis 1–3 we are told that we are created in God's image. We are designed by the Creator to be relational, rational, and responsible. We were created to know our Creator and to live in relationship with Him and others. We can understand and respond to the revelation of God and ultimately we will be held accountable for our response to our Creator.

The name Elohim assures us that our life has purpose and meaning. Have you come to know your Creator as your Redeemer? He is the Creator of all that exists and He loves you.

Adonai

Second, we looked at the name Adonai in Genesis 15:1–8 in conjunction with the faith pilgrimage of Abraham. The story of Abraham's life begins with God's call and His promise of a blessing. In Genesis 12:2 we are told that God promised that He would make Abraham a great nation and that He would make His name great. In Genesis 15 we take up the story after Lot, the nephew of Abraham, has been rescued from Sodom and Gommorah.

The word of the Lord came to Abraham in a vision confirming His promise to Abraham and declaring that He is a shield to him. Abraham responds with a level of despair since he has no children. He suggests that Eliezer, his servant, is his only heir. God again assures Abraham that his heir will come from his own body and that his descendants will be more numerous than the stars. In Genesis 15:2, Abraham addresses God as Adonai Jehovah. (Jehovah is the name we studied in Exodus 3.) Here our focus is on the confession that Jehovah is Abraham's Adonai. The word *adonai* means "master" or "Lord." The primary significance of that name is to declare that God is the Owner of all that is. Since God is Lord, He can rightly require our obedience.

Adonai means complete possession, and it signifies our complete surrender. When Abraham surrendered his will to Sovereign God, God revealed Himself as a master who declares His ability and intention to meet his every need. We found the same name in Exodus 4:10 when Moses was commissioned to deliver Israel from Egyptian bondage. He addressed God as Adonai, thus acknowledging God's absolute right to send him wherever He desired. We also understand that He is a loving and powerful Master who never asks us to do something that He has not created and empowered us to do.

You will find three distinct characteristics about those who have learned the significance of calling God their Lord:

1. They acknowledge themselves as servants. Paul often referred to himself as a bondslave. He joyfully and willingly placed Himself at God's disposal.

2. Servants understand that God is a loving and wholly sufficient Master.

3. They realize that, because of His sufficiency, they can do whatever He has called them to do. In other words, there is a sort

of holy boldness. I often hear Christians who decry their inability to witness or serve. What they have failed to understand is the sufficiency of the One they call Lord.

El Elyon

In Genesis 14:20, we discovered the beautiful name El Elyon, "God most high," through our continued study of the life of Abraham. Abraham's nephew Lot had chosen the land where he would settle by sight and not by faith. Lot had taken his family and belongings and had moved into the area of Sodom and Gommorrah. The city-states in that area had rebelled against their servitude to Chedorlaomer. Chedorlaomer and his alliance won the battle and the defeated people fled into the hill country. This story of the rebellion of the city-states would have little significance to the biblical story if Lot and his family had not been among the captives.

Abraham marshals his forces and liberates his nephew. When Abraham returns as the victorious liberator, he is met by two different kings. One is the king of Sodom, who wants to negotiate a deal with Abraham. He suggests that Abraham can keep all the spoils of war if he will simply return to him all his servants. The humorous part of the story is that the king of Sodom had nothing to bargain with. He had nothing to offer Abraham. He was a defeated king.

The second king to meet Abraham is Melchizedek, who is introduced as king of Salem and a priest of God Most High (Gen. 14:18). Melchizedek requests nothing of Abraham, but rather blesses Abraham in the name of God Most High who is the Possessor of heaven and earth. Melchizedek declares that God has delivered his enemies into Abraham's hands. Abraham gladly and submissively gives the king of Salem a tenth of all the spoils of war.

Abraham then turns to the king of Sodom and declares, "I have sworn to the LORD God Most High, possessor of heaven and earth, that I will not take a thread or a sandal thong or anything that is yours, lest you should say, 'I have made Abram rich'" (vv. 22b–23).

When we utter the name El Elyon, we are declaring that God Most High has all the resources of heaven and earth available to Him and that He alone can supply our need. He alone is sufficient. Have you discovered that God is El Elyon, sufficient to supply your every need?

El Shaddai

The name El Shaddai is translated "God Almighty" or "God almighty to nourish." Once again, we see the significance of the name through the growing faith relationship of Abraham. In Genesis 17:1–2, we find a ninety-nine-year-old man who is still struggling to believe that God can fulfill His promise to develop from him a mighty nation. You will recall that he had already suggested to God that Eliezer, his servant, could be his heir. Later, he took Sarah's advice and fathered a child by her handmaiden. The son, Ishmael, and his descendants became a constant thorn to Israel. These fleshly attempts to accomplish the purpose of God were fundamentally sins of unbelief.

The name El Shaddai was a word of reassurance that God was indeed almighty to nourish and to fulfill His covenant promise. The lesson we need to learn as we voice the name El Shaddai is that we are totally insufficient in our own strength, but God is fully sufficient. By faith we place ourselves in the hands of God, who can bring forth life in a barren womb.

Jehovah Jireh

In Genesis 22, we come to the final step, the last hurdle, in the faith-building pilgrimage of Abraham. The child of promise, Isaac, has been provided by El Shaddai. God calls Abraham to take his son Isaac to Mt. Moriah and offer him as a sacrifice. The drama of the story is unsurpassed in Scripture. Abraham and Isaac leave the servants and walk alone to the mountain of sacrifice. Isaac bears the wood that will kindle the fire to consume the sacrifice. When he inquires about the lamb for the sacrifice, Abraham's faith response is that the Lord Himself will provide the lamb for the sacrifice.

The scene is set as the lad is bound and laid upon the wood and Abraham is poised with knife in hand, prepared to sacrifice his only beloved son. The angel of the Lord stops the proceedings and Abraham replaces his son with a ram caught in a nearby thicket. God tells Abraham that He is Jehovah Jireh, the Lord will provide.

We can know that God is our Provider. He can supply every need that we encounter. We can also be assured that we can trust God with our most treasured possession. When we lay that which we value most on the altar of sacrifice, God will raise it up. What in your life are you afraid to release? Are you struggling with finances and afraid to tithe? Are you clinging to your own sense of security and anxious about retirement? You can be assured that Jehovah Jireh can provide.

Jehovah (Yahweh)

The great memorial name of God is given to Moses at the burning bush in Exodus 3. The people of Israel were languishing in Egyptian bondage. God speaks to Moses, first identifying Himself as the God of Abraham, Isaac, and Jacob. The God that had mightily worked in the past was speaking to Moses in the present. God declares that He is aware of the suffering of His people and has determined to come down and deliver them. Moses is enthusiastic about the announcement until he discovers that he is to be the human instrument through whom God brings deliverance.

Moses begins to make excuses about his inability. He argues that he is not a gifted communicator. He tells God that the people will not believe that God has sent him. Moses argues that the people will ask about God's name. What is he to say then? God declares that He is "I AM WHO I AM," the name Jehovah or Yahweh, which is to be His memorial name forever. The word translated "I Am who I Am" is actually the imperfect stem of the verb "to be." As such, it indicates incomplete action. It is often translated in the future tense, but it can be used to denote any type of action that is not complete. This action may have started in the past and continue in the present, but it is not yet finished. God's power seen in the past in and through the lives of the patriarchs was available to Moses in the present. His miraculous power was not to be confined to the past; it could be known in the present and extend into the future.

The ever-living God who reveals Himself to His covenant people as an unchanging God will be faithful to His covenant. The name Jehovah introduces God's moral and spiritual attributes. He is a covenant God who promises to redeem Israel.

Today we need to experience God as active in our present tense. Too many of us confine God to the pages of biblical revelation and are afraid to allow Him to act in and through their lives today. When called upon to serve or bear witness, we frequently argue with the God who created us and wants to indwell and empower us through His Spirit.

Jehovah Rophe

God delivered Israel from their Egyptian bondage, providing safe passage through the Red Sea. Not long after their songs of victory died out, they began to grumble and complain about the lack of food and water. Finally there appears before them a promise of provision. They find water at Marah, but the water is bitter and not safe for consumption.

Moses cried out to the Lord and He instructed Moses to throw a tree into the water. The waters immediately became sweet and God satisfied the people's thirst. God told Israel that if they would pay earnest heed to the voice of the Lord, do what is right in His sight, and keep His statutes, that He would not put upon them the diseases that had afflicted the Egyptians. He then declares that He is the Healer, Jehovah Rophe. Not long after these events, Israel arrived at Elim, where they found twelve springs of water and seventy date palms (Exod. 15:22–27).

My wife, our baby daughter, and I were preparing to leave England after three years in graduate school at Cambridge. I had been offered a job teaching Greek when I returned to the United States. We thought the job would provide a wonderful opportunity to transition back to life in the States and provide us with financial security while I sought a pastoral position. Security was especially important to us, because my wife was expecting our second daughter. At the last moment, the job offer was withdrawn and the letter of rejection arrived just months before I was to submit my dissertation and we were to return to the U.S. We could have allowed that experience to cause us to be bitter. We could have blamed the administration of the school or even God for letting us down. Instead, we found that God had cast Himself into our lives in such a way that He turned our disappointment into joy. He became for us Jehovah Rophe. Our Marah became Elim.

You can trust God to enter the most difficult and challenging experiences of your life and turn bitterness to sweetness. He is a Lord who wants to bring healing.

Jehovah Nissi

As we continue to follow the wilderness journey of the people of God, we travel to Rephidim. The people of Israel are confronted by the descendants of Amalek. The Amalekites often represent the power of evil in Scripture. Israel is forced to go to war against this more powerful and organized army. Moses, as commander-in-chief, stations himself on top of the hill with the rod of God in his hand. The Bible tells us that when he held the rod aloft, Israel prevailed, but when he let his arm down, Amalek prevailed. With the assistance of Aaron and Hur, Moses was able to keep his hands steady until the sun set and Joshua and his army prevailed. Moses built an altar at that place and named it Jehovah Nissi, the Lord is my Banner.

We briefly looked at another banner held aloft by Moses. In Numbers 21, we find the children of Israel in a difficult predicament. They are being bitten by venomous snakes. The people cry out to Moses to ask God to remove the serpents from them. God instructs Moses to make a bronze serpent and place it on a standard and to instruct the people that if they look upon the standard after being bitten, they would live. Obviously, there was no healing power in a piece of bronze on a stick. Their rescue came from the Lord, who instructed them to look in faith to Him for their redemption.

Jesus used this story in His interview with Nicodemus in John 3. "'And as Moses lifted up the serpent in the wilderness, even so must the Son of Man be lifted up; that whoever believes, may in Him have eternal life'" (John 3:14–15). In our minds the serpent has always represented evil. In the Garden of Eden, we find the cursing of the serpent who tempts Eve. We find it somewhat objectionable that Jesus likens His death on the cross to the lifting up of the serpent in the wilderness. But isn't that precisely the point of the cross? Paul tells us that He who knew no sin became sin that we might be the righteousness of God in Him (2 Cor. 5:21). Jesus became the ultimate Banner of deliverance and victory.

You can call upon God as Jehovah Nissi, your Banner of victory, as you enter the realm of spiritual conflict on a daily basis. When you come under attack by others, you need not defend yourself, but stand under the Banner of Jehovah Nissi. When you find yourself struggling with temptation and the power of evil, stand under Jehovah Nissi.

Jehovah Mekadesh

In the beautiful Book of Leviticus, we found the name Jehovah Mekadesh, the God who sanctifies. Here, once again, we note that God has revealed Himself in such a manner as to meet the growing needs and understanding of His people. The Book of Leviticus is the book of spiritual life as it prescribes the walk and worship of the people of God. This name describes the essential character of God. The holiness of God integrates the other wonderful attributes we have discovered about God.

The central truth behind this name is that God is holy and thus desires to sanctify His people. What does this mean functionally? First, it means that we are set apart for service to a holy

God. I can't think of anything that is more exciting than the discovery that God gives us the privilege to serve Him. In Romans 12:1–2, we are told to offer our bodies as living sacrifices, which is our reasonable act of service. In that same passage, we discover the wonderful truth that this gift of service has already been declared good, acceptable, and perfect. Isn't it exhilarating to know that you can serve the living God in an acceptable way? This great truth gives us a clear sense of purpose. God created us to serve Him and through His grace we can be set apart for that service.

Our sanctification also means that we are to be pure and holy vessels. If we are going to be used powerfully and effectively by God, we need to be clean vessels. There are areas of behavior and sins of the flesh and the spirit that need to be avoided. We must say no to sin. The Bible often uses the analogy of putting off sin the way one would strip off soiled garments. As you call upon the name Jehovah Mekadesh, remember that God has called you to serve Him and to live like light in the midst of a dark world.

Jehovah Shalom

Approximately two hundred years had passed since the giving of the name Jehovah Mekadesh in Leviticus. The Promised Land had been inhabited and divided among the twelve tribes. Israel had no cohesive government, virtually no unity, and in spite of Moses' warnings, they had turned to other gods. They had lost their spiritual vision and had fallen prey to their appetites.

When you read the Book of Judges, you will find a cyclical pattern of life. Israel sins, that sin is followed by judgment and punishment that in turn is followed by repentance and God's deliverance. Unfortunately, Israel was slow to learn the lesson and they lived in this cyclical pattern.

Many Christians today find themselves in a similar situation when it comes to their own spiritual walk. They make a commitment to Christ and are born again. They enter that "promised land" experience with great joy and enthusiasm. Then they begin to compromise, they lose their spiritual focus, and sin dulls their relationship with God. God, out of His great love, brings discipline to His children, and we experience the punishment for our sin. Out of our grief we cry out for forgiveness and God is faithful to forgive our sin and cleanse us of our unrighteousness. But here's the question we long to answer: How can we break free of this repetitious cycle that keeps us from productive service? The name Jehovah Shalom gives us great hope.

In Judges 6, we find the wonderful story of Gideon. Because of their sin, the Lord gave Israel into the hands of the Midianites for seven years. God's messenger appears to Gideon and commissions him to deliver Israel. Gideon considers himself unworthy of the task and argues that his family is the least in Manasseh and he is the youngest in his family. Gideon does have two questions for the messenger of God. If God is for us, why are we experiencing such devastation? Second, he inquires about the absence of the sort of miracles their ancestors had experienced.

God's response is the calling and commissioning of Gideon. Gideon wants some assurance that God will be with him and requests a sign from God. Once Gideon is convinced that he has seen the messenger of the Lord face-to-face, he is frightened for his life. The Lord assures him that he will experience peace and not death. In response, Gideon builds an altar and names it Jehovah Shalom.

The idea behind the word *shalom* is wholeness and harmony in relationship with God. Peace is the deepest desire and need of the human heart. When you find yourself wondering where is the blessing of God's presence in your life, you need to remember that He is Jehovah Shalom. He desires to bring peace if you will simply return to Him.

Jehovah Tsidkenu

In Jeremiah 23:1–6, we discover that the Lord is our Righteousness. We enter the historical narrative when the kingdom of Judah was on the brink of collapse. Nearly one hundred years before, the ten tribes of Israel had been taken into captivity, but Judah had apparently learned little from the demise of the northern tribes. Still, there had been rays of hope in their turbulent history. The good king Josiah restored worship as the Word of God was rediscovered. The effects of the revival soon wore off, though, and spiritual decline once again became the norm.

As the moral and material decay became evident, the prophet Jeremiah predicted the captivity of Judah. He pronounced judgment on the shepherds who were destroying and scattering the sheep of God's pasture. Yet there is a word of hope. Through Jeremiah, God declared that He would raise up shepherds that would tend the flock and remove their fear. Further, Jeremiah indicates that the Lord had promised to raise up for David a righteous branch to reign as king and His name will be the Lord our Righteousness.

It would be impossible for us to read about this wonderful name and not think of our precious Lord Jesus, who was the Righteous Branch of David and who now reigns as King. You can be assured that you have a righteous Lord who will tend His flock. You do not need to give in to fear, because Christ is your Righteous Lord.

Jehovah Rohi

Although some Bible teachers might not include Jehovah Rohi as a distinctive name for God, the image has such appeal to us that we couldn't omit it. The name is taken from Psalm 23 and depicts the Lord as Shepherd. The psalm was written by David in the latter years of his life, which had been marked by exhilarating victories and depressing defeats. His sin of immorality had a tragic impact on his family. Through it all, though, David had a heart for God and discovered that He was a gentle Shepherd.

It is fascinating that David the warrior goes back to those childhood memories emerging from his own experience as a shepherd. He writes about a God who can lead to good pasture and still waters. He has experienced what it was like to know the presence of the Shepherd as he walked through the valley of the shadow of death. He had been comforted by the protective presence of His rod and staff.

You can be assured that God is your Shepherd when you are struggling in your job, when you are dealing with strained or broken relationships. You can be assured that He will walk with you through the dark valleys of your life. You can know that you will dwell in the house of the Lord forever. Do you remember how the disciples felt when Jesus told them of His impending death? He reassured them that in His Father's house were many mansions and that He was going to prepare a place for them. Jesus is the Good Shepherd who laid down His life for the sheep.

Jehovah Shammah

The final name, Jehovah Shammah, was found in Ezekiel 48:35. Ezekiel brings a word of hope out of a shattering experience of captivity. The destruction of Jerusalem and the temple had been a crushing blow to Jewish pride. The faith of Israel was distinguished by its emphasis on the presence of God in their midst. They had a visible symbol of His presence in the pillar of cloud and fire. The movable tabernacle, the ark, and finally the temple were indicative of God's presence. Now, with the temple destroyed and the people in captivity, they had found joyous worship to be a challenge.

Ezekiel prophesies about a day of restoration where there will be a new city of Zion that shall be called "the Lord is there." God's presence will be the focal point of this city. We saw the first level of fulfillment of the promise of Jehovah Shammah in the opening pages of Matthew's Gospel that declared the birth of Immanuel, "God with us." God's presence and His glory were tabernacled among men in the person of Jesus Christ. Jesus told His disciples that if they had seen Him they had seen the Father.

Second, we discovered that God wants His church to express His presence fully. It is the Father's desire that the church express His fullness even as Jesus expressed His fullness. Jesus prayed that His disciples might have unity, joy, and purity, because the glory of God, which had been present in Him, was now to be present through them. We sometimes forget that we represent the presence of Holy God.

Finally, we looked to the ultimate fulfillment of Ezekiel's prophecy in Revelation 21. John looks into the future and sees a new Jerusalem and a new temple. This one will not be constructed with bricks and mortar. This one will not need the sun for light, because the Lamb will provide its illumination. This city will not have sorrow or death or pain. The key component of this city is the continual and eternal presence of God.

FINAL REFLECTIONS

I grew up in the foothills of the Blue Ridge Mountains. I have always enjoyed excursions down the Blue Ridge Parkway. It is breathtaking in the fall when God paints the mountains with His full palette of colors. At the first overlook, we always pull over and marvel at the beauty and sometimes we would say aloud, "It can't get any more beautiful than this." Then we pile back into the car and we ascend further up the mountains and pull over once again to discover that the view has become even more breathtaking.

When I was pastor at First Baptist in Norfolk, one of my favorite services was our Thanksgiving morning worship service. It began with a church-wide pancake breakfast and concluded with a worship experience. We placed microphones throughout the sanctuary and invited people to share a word of thanks. It became a tradition to have my dad preach the Thanksgiving service. Dad faithfully pastored small North Carolina churches for the fifty-five years of his ministry. He told me of his desire to preach to a large congregation and thus we joyfully filled the sanctuary to hear him preach every Thanksgiving.

My minister of music, Larry White, said that if I were going to invite my dad to preach, he wanted to invite his dad to sing. I told him that I thought it would be an honor to have him sing. Larry's dad lived in Winston-Salem and, coincidentally, the first time he was to join us for Thanksgiving, he rode to Norfolk in our family van. His somewhat aging but still rich tenor voice serenaded us all the way to town. When he stood to sing that Thanksgiving morning, he sang the same song. As I looked upon those two great heroes of the faith, I heard the musical testimony, "The longer I serve Him, the sweeter He grows." Have you discovered this to be true in your walk with God? At each vista of the faith journey, you discover that the glory of the Lord becomes ever more magnificent.

I hope this study of the names of God has been like a drive up the Blue Ridge Parkway and that at each stop you have found the view of God's majesty has been more breathtaking. We began with the Creator and we concluded with the God who is eternally present with His people. My heart's desire in writing this book is that you would come to know the God who speaks. To know God, you must come to Him through His Son, Jesus. Jesus declared that He is the Way, the Truth, and the Life, and that no man can come to the Father except through Him. Jesus was the final and full revelation of God. Jesus is fully God and thus it should not surprise us that each of the names of God leads us to Jesus.

If you are already a Christian, I pray that this study will lead you to a more intimate relationship with the Father. I hope you will find the names of God helpful in your prayer life as you voice those names as the needs of your life dictate. I pray that you will experience His sufficiency and live abundantly in His presence.